WHO'S ON YOUR *Board*

Six Steps to Curating *Your Personal Board of Directors*

Stacy L. Gomes, EdD, MEd

Leena S. Guptha, DO, MBA, PhD

Foreword by Shamini Jain, PhD

WHO'S ON YOUR BOARD?
Six Steps to Curating Your Personal Board of Directors

Book Design by Transcendent Publishing

ISBN: 979-8-9992030-8-3

This publication is intended as a valuable resource for readers; however, it is not a substitute for professional advice. If expert guidance is required, the services of a qualified professional should be sought.

Printed in the United States of America.

DEDICATION

This book is dedicated to all the people who want to grow a little bit each day and to those who dare to make their better selves a reality.

To my family—my daughter DeLanie Skye Gomes, who has always been the inspiration for me to be a better mom, friend and human, her father Tommy (Fishmonger) Gomes who has always been a role model for hard work and the hustle, and my father Roger Lawson, who at the age of eighty-nine, still inspires me to be physically active riding bikes and diving!

—From Stacy

This book, all that has come before it, and all that will follow is dedicated to my wise, spiritual, and loving mother Rita (R.I.P.). She taught me to live a life of positive affirmation and growth mindset, reflected as core pillars of *Who's on Your Board,* and to my father, Tim, who through the *Wheel of Life* transformed his life in personal growth and well-being, starting at age 80 and is thriving at 92.

—From Leena

TABLE OF CONTENTS

FOREWORD

by
Shamini Jain, PhD

There are moments in our lives when we feel the quiet whisper of our deeper knowing—the sense that there is more to us, more for us, and more available to us than what we can see on the surface. Yet even as we yearn to grow into our fullness, we forget a simple, sacred truth: we do not grow alone. We grow in relationship.

Every healing tradition, every spiritual lineage, every genuine path of awakening reminds us that we are woven into a glowing tapestry of consciousness—one that expands through connection, intention, and love. Modern science simply gives new language to what our ancestors already understood: our biology, our emotions, and our very sense of self are shaped through the people who walk beside us.

This is why the idea of a Personal Board of Directors is far more than a practical exercise. It is a call to consciously tend the garden of your life. It is an invitation to choose, with thoughtfulness and reverence, the souls who will water the seeds of your becoming and remind you of your wholeness when you forget.

Biofield science teaches us that we do not thrive in isolation, and that healing and growth do not emerge from will – they emerge from resonance. When we stand in the presence of those who embody clarity, compassion, wisdom, and integrity, our own field begins to shift and lift. We entrain to coherence. We soften. We heal. We expand.

And so, the question becomes: Who do you invite into your field? Who sits at the table of your becoming?

Who's On Your Board? answers this question with a rare blend of heart, insight, and grounded wisdom. Dr. Stacy Gomes and Dr. Leena Guptha offer a loving structure that honors the multidimensional nature of healing. Through the Wheel of Life, they guide you to see your life as a whole, interconnected ecosystem—one in which each area deserves tending, nourishment, and support.

What moves me most about this book is its invitation into conscious choice. You are not simply gathering advisors—you are weaving a circle of resonance. You are choosing, with intention, the voices you wish to echo through your mind, the energies you want reflected in your body, and the wisdom you want guiding your spirit.

This is the art of healing: to surround yourself not only with those who uplift you, but with those who remind you of the truth and beauty of your own soul's expression, so that you can become and create more than your egoic will could ever imagine.

As you step into the journey these pages offer, may you do so with tenderness and curiosity. May the board you create help you not only navigate your challenges but also awaken your joy, your purpose, and your deepest sense of connection. And may this circle of support become a living expression of the truth that has always been yours:

You are connected.

You are supported.

You are never alone on the path of your becoming.

—Shamini Jain, PhD
Founder and President, Consciousness and Healing Initiative (CHI)
Adjunct Professor, UC San Diego
Scientist, psychologist, and author of Healing Ourselves

INTRODUCTION

If you're a self-starter seeking more purpose and balance, we have written this book entirely for you. By the end, you will have all you need to create your ideal personal board of directors through our *Wheel of Life* approach—your one-way ticket to finding balance without sacrificing quality of life in one area to find success in another.

I have been an educational pioneer leading some of the nation's best-known complementary, alternative, mainstream, and integrative medicine schools, organizations, and clinical sites, focusing on body, mind, and spirit for over twenty-five years. I have a doctorate in leadership and have taught leadership to thousands of students, faculty, and colleagues. The foundation of my work and passion in life is self-care for body, mind, and spirit. I try to teach my students, family, and friends that we thrive best when we take care of ourselves first. My mission is to be a role model for health, education, and leadership, and this is, and will remain my "true north."

One of the books I required in my class was *True North* by Bill George. Bill George is an executive fellow at Harvard Business School where he also taught leadership courses for eighteen years. He's the former board chairman and CEO of the healthcare technology company Medtronic and was also a senior executive at Honeywell. He's authored several books centered on his True North philosophy. Bill argues that it's not about being the most talented, or the most charming person in the boardroom, it's about being true to yourself and staying focused on your core priorities and values—what he calls your unique "True North" and what you will see makes up your *Wheel of Life*.

Bill is a very successful businessman and has a regular seventy-five-minute meeting every Wednesday with a group that was founded thirty years ago. In fact, Bill and his gang consider the group to be one of the most important elements of life. It helps them clarify their beliefs, values, and views on important issues;

Dr. Stacy and Bill George

they give each other the necessary feedback and suggestions. Together, they have created their own personal board of directors! Bill has been one of my "secret" board members for many years guiding me in personal and professional growth. I am privileged to know him through my role as a board member of the Academy of Integrative Health and Medicine and will forever be grateful for his generous leadership in demonstrating what true success can look like.

Friends and family members often comment on my success, and I believe I have achieved success but not in the way it's traditionally defined. Yes, I have a great career, education, financial stability, health, and motherhood, but these do not make up my definition of success and wellbeing. The reason I feel successful lies in one accomplishment: finding balance. Ironically, this accomplishment often seems much more elusive and unattainable than all of the others combined. This was the case for me as well.

For years, I was seeking balance in all areas of my life—like yin and yang and the gentle submission of Tai Chi push hands. You must push forward in one area while yielding to greater forces out of your control in other areas. This is how you can finally create balance and stop neglecting certain parts of your life to maintain your success in another.

I was a single parent raising my daughter alone which meant many days of not knowing how I was going to pay the bills or keep food on the table and a roof over our heads. I was not raised with generational wealth, so I worked hard to put myself through three undergraduate, graduate, and doctoral degrees and was very focused on my career. Like far too many of us, I was out of balance many times over the years—sometimes at the expense of self-care and failing to focus on the full *Wheel of Life*. It took me years to master the skill of wellbeing and balance, and so can you.

Too many people are narrowly focused on financial and career success, sometimes out of necessity, but many times out of sheer neglect for maintaining the wheels on their bus. Self-growth means recognizing the areas of your life in need of attention, so your wheels aren't wonky!

Real success begins with balance and intentional self-care. This book's perspective is based on the fact that I have sought to balance the *Wheel of Life* by seeking out individuals and information that fill gaps in my knowledge and self-care. This may involve hearing things we don't want to hear but *need* to hear or stepping back and learning from role models who have wisdom in areas you'd like to learn more about. I continue to move the right people onto my bus by creating my personal board of directors, and you can too!

When I was in my doctoral program for educational leadership, one of my required books was *Good to Great* by Jim Collins. Out of all our required books, this was the one that always stuck with me. Over the years, I have learned that we all collect people for our bus ride, whether we know it or not. It wasn't clear at the time that getting the right people on the bus was pivotal to creating your own personal board of directors.

This book is about how to be intentional with regard to who's on your bus—*or board*. I have used this with my own students, family, and friends and now see how important it is to reassess who is sitting on the bus and possibly move some of those people on (or off) the bus to truly prioritize your own growth.

"Look, I don't really know where we should take this bus. But I know this much: If we get the right people on the bus, the right people in the right seats, and the wrong people off the bus, then we'll figure out how to take it someplace great." Jim Collins

Getting the right people on your bus requires intentional self-awareness that is part of creating your personal board of directors—self-awareness that involves knowing what strengths are needed on your bus and then building it accordingly. I am fortunate to be surrounded by national leaders in health care and education who are focused on transformation at many levels. Many of my friends and colleagues are authors, and *The Pebble in the Pond* published by Duke Integrative Leadership states the importance of building a personal board of advisors. Even though *The Pebble in the Pond* is written for health care leaders, the message applies to everyone. I have just substituted board "members" for "advisors."

—Stacy

---

[1] *Illustration courtesy of Snyder Law*

Creating a Personal Board of Advisors

With informed mindfulness comes an understanding of one's strengths and weaknesses. No one can be an expert in all things, and even a leader's strongest areas can always be strengthened further. However, a crucial part of personal development comes through addressing the areas in which one is challenged. It's all about self-awareness.

Executive coach and leadership development expert Michael Aquilino suggests that integrative leaders should assess their strengths and weaknesses and, by identifying individuals who can help them in their development and growth, build a personal board of advisors.

We are the protagonists of the movie that is our life, the authors of the chapters that make up our lives, and we need personal board members to help us lead an effective journey. This book was created to help YOU create your dream movie or craft the next several chapters in the book of your life. This book comes from decades of seeking wisdom from those deceased and alive on how to improve life.

This book was conceived after many years of teaching leadership to doctoral students. I required each student to develop a personal mission and vision, and my message to them was simple: **You can't lead others if you can't be the leader of your own life.** Being a leader of your own life requires intentional self-care in many areas—what we call the *Wheel of Life*.

We all have an area in our lives that we want to be better at. This book is how we do that, sometimes intuitively and sometimes with some conscious, intentional planning.

At the root of this awareness are the nuanced strategies I've used to curate a unique board of directors. I turn to these individuals (some of them "secret") for the latest information, for checks and balances, to confirm understandings, for review strategies, for the times when

I need someone to push me harder than I would on my own, and the times I need someone to call me out when I don't even see that I've strayed.

I have had the benefit of valuable insight from my good friend and former academic dean and one of my personal board members Dr. Leena Guptha. Dr. Leena, as she is known, has contributed greatly with her focused feedback and expertise in growth mindset. She has skillfully co-written this book knowing how strongly a growth mindset contributes to self-improvement. Dr. Leena is a beacon of positive affirmations and a reminder that we can change 80% of negative thoughts we have in a day (which often add up to over *70,000*) by simply modifying our self-talk. (Huffington Post).

> I've been an integrative health practitioner and educator across my various professions (osteopathic medicine, naturopathic medicine, acupuncture, hypnotherapy, and coaching) and other health professions (massage therapy, nursing, chiropractic, physical therapy) for over three decades. The inspiration for my journey came from seeing my mother struggle with auto-immune disease but more so utilizing the then-called "alternative medicines" together with modern inventions, and she lived thirty years beyond her medical prognosis. This personal experience led me on a Mission to educate and inspire a global community as to the value of personal peak performance, health, and happiness through innovative solutions 2B well for life. My mother was a role model of growth mindset, and I keep her spirit alive through serving others to live their best life.
>
> **Growth Mindset:** My mother was a person who lived a life challenged by health conditions. We were told she would not live beyond the age of forty, at which time I

would have been fourteen. She was a spiritual, intuitive, naturally insightful, wise person who wanted to ensure that if she passed in my teens, I would have tools for a values-based life.

She often said: *Make decisions for happiness and the rest will fall into place.*

Through her struggles of pain and immobility, I was always amazed how she kept a smile on her face, saw the glass half full, and often encouraged me to seek out the silver lining and nurture a positive and growth mindset. As my father recently said, "She believed all things were possible."

The Advent of Secret Board Members: Before the world was even talking about whole health, integrative medicine, and living a balanced life, my journey with my mother Rita (RIP) led me to co-creating her health goals, navigating our daily life realities, and attempting to move forward the best we could with our acquired education of health, life, and mindset. From the time I was seven, my mother was hospitalized for months at a time. *I lived with different families on and off for the next decade and developed my "secret board members" just to get by.*

Enter the *Wheel of Life*: In many ways, I was living the life of an adult in my childhood, driven to extend my mother's longevity beyond the expected forty years. My mother wanted to be sure I understood factors of the prevention of disease, which led to a deep understanding and much discussion with her (often while she lay in bed) of what today we call the *Wheel of Life*. I spent much of my teenage years reading, exploring, and appreciating a whole health approach to life and living its implementation at home.

A Mission-Driven Path: When I was seventeen, I met with the high school career counselor who predetermined marine biology and biochemistry to be my future! My earlier dreams (ages four to seven) were to be the first female engineer, designing and building bridges. However, by age seventeen, I felt an undeniable force to serve those like my mother to reach their optimal health. I let my counselor know I would be pursuing osteopathic medicine, naturopathic medicine, and acupuncture for at least a decade and probably further studies around health and life management. Needless to say, he was not impressed, and we never met again … Since then, my mission and vision changed little in the following four decades (reflected in Chapter 4 where we talk about creating goals.)

This book is a reflection that provides you with learning and a deeper awareness to live your authentic life of self-care and achieve goals and dreams through secret and mindfully chosen directors of YOUR board. Be the author of the BOOK OF YOUR LIFE. You are the main actor in the movie of the life you live … Make it count!

—From Dr. Leena

This is a highly personal journey of my lack of satisfaction with trying to find the one strategy or the one person with the "answers." As my questions broadened in many more areas beyond career and financial success, I was creating my own personal board of directors to lean on for wisdom.

Are you ready to see how to create your own personal board of directors? This book will walk you through a six-step process for curating your board and focused self-improvement because you are the CEO of your life!

> **Step 1:** Make a list of people you look up to who have succeeded in something that impresses you.
>
> **Step 2:** Identify "secret" board members—people you know or follow who will help you improve.
>
> **Step 3:** Complete the *Wheel of Life* and identify a category you want to focus on.
>
> **Step 4:** Identify your board members for each area of your *Wheel of Life.*
>
> **Step 5:** Create a growth mindset to attract the right board members.
>
> **Step 6:** Make contact with potential board members and describe what area they might help with.

Chapter 1

WHY WE NEED A PERSONAL BOARD OF DIRECTORS

*"Renewal is the principle—and the process—that empowers
us to move on an upward spiral of growth and change,
of continuous improvement."*

—Dr. Stephen R. Covey

Aren't we all trying to improve ourselves in some areas of our lives each day, week, or year? How many people spend time and thought on "New Year's Resolutions?" Whether it's earning more money, getting more active, eating better—the list of resolutions is endless. When we talk to friends about this book, most end up realizing that they wish they had their own board of directors to help improve their lives. When we ask them why they don't, no one seems to have a good answer. Most tilt their head with a quiet questioning gaze, indicating they have never thought about it or don't know how to start.

Some tell us that they have mentors or coaches, but they play different roles than board members, and we'll compare them in Chapter 3. Who do you lean on to improve in areas that don't relate to your career, but your own self-improvement and personal goals? Do you have a system, process, or plan to "sharpen your saw," or are you just winging it, hoping you get better as time goes on? If YOU haven't chosen your board, your board will choose you!

You are responsible for creating your own growth and carving out a successful life. You are also the primary decision-maker in your life. This is why our *Wheel of Life* approach encourages you to *think of yourself as your own business* with you at the helm as CEO (Chief Empowerment Officer). And just like big organizations and non-profits have a board of directors who hold the CEO accountable as a steward and guardian of the business assets, key decisions, and investments, you can develop a similar concept to support your own life.

Being the CEO of your life involves taking full control and being responsible for your own future. It requires you to be strategic and diligent about ongoing self-development and growth. It also means recognizing your value and investing in yourself so that you can continue to position yourself as an asset for yourself and others.

Unfortunately, most people are treading water or adrift without a rudder when trying to improve their lives. Most people don't think of themselves as a business, organization, or project, so they have not thought about the usefulness of a personal board of directors. They may have a mentor or coach for one area of their lives, but when it comes to their own self-care or other goals that have been put on the back burner, they lack the right advocate. The intentional process of creating a team, or board of directors, to help you improve your life can be achieved, and this book will give you the six-step process to create the board you didn't know you needed.

Abraham Maslow's "Hierarchy of Needs" pyramid organizes human needs from the most basic (physiological) to the most advanced (self-actualization). In the present age of instant gratification and abundance, some people stagnate on the lower rungs of Maslow's hierarchy because it's within their comfort zone. Others, on the other hand, remain trapped below their full potential because they try to ascend too quickly or skip steps along the way. This is where a comprehensive support system comes in.

In chapter one, you'll learn how strategically building a personal board is so effective for manifesting a life full of potential. You'll also learn the difference between a traditional board of directors and a personal board of directors. Each chapter will provide examples of successful friends who have personal board members and how they use our process. Finally, each chapter will prompt you with action items to help move you toward curating your own board in a simple six-step process!

The famous author Paulo Coelho is a Brazilian lyricist and novelist famous for his book *The Alchemist*. Coelho's parents committed him to a mental institution from which he escaped three times before being released at the age of twenty. Coelho later remarked:

> "It wasn't that they wanted to hurt me, but they didn't know what to do … They did not do that to destroy me, they did that to save me."

In 1986 Coelho walked the 500-plus mile Road of Santiago de Compostela in northwestern Spain. On the path, he had a spiritual awakening, which he describes in *The Pilgrimage*:

> "Everyone is capable of these things. And though no one thinks of themselves as a warrior of light, we all are."

A warrior of light knows that he has much to be grateful for. His gratitude, however, is not limited to the spiritual world; he never forgets his friends, for their blood mingled with his on the battlefield. A warrior does not need to be reminded of the help given him by others; he is the first to remember and makes sure to share with them any rewards he receives.

The Ninja warriors go to the field where some wheat has just been planted. Obeying the trainer's command, they jump over the places where the seeds were sown. Every day the Ninja warriors return to the field. The seeds turn into buds, and the warriors jump over them. The buds turn into small plants, and the warriors jump over them. They do not become bored. They do not feel it is a waste of time. The wheat grows, and the jumps become higher and higher. In this way, when the plant is ripe, the Ninja warriors still manage to jump over it. Why? As a result of their jumping over what many may have seen as insignificant, has allowed them to be keenly aware of their obstacles.

—Paulo Coelho,
Manual of the Warrior of the Light

The hard part of being a warrior of light is the ongoing work needed to sharpen the saw. Think of this book and your board members as trainers to help you sharpen the saw. "Sharpen the Saw" is synonymous with "self-care" or "self-renewal," which we observe many friends, family members and patients struggle with.

When I was in my doctoral program, we had hundreds of required and recommended books. Although most sit on shelves or in boxes and rarely get opened, there are a few that I reach for repeatedly to remind myself to continue to sharpen the saw.

—From Stacy

Sharpening the Saw

Stephen Covey's book *The 7 Habits of Highly Effective People* is one of those books that continues to stand the test of time. I not only use it daily but expand on it with my practice of putting the right people on my board.

7 HABITS OF HIGHLY EFFECTIVE PEOPLE

1 BE PROACTIVE
Focus on your circle of influence.
Take responsibility for your reactioris s
your experiences.

2 BEGIN WITH THE END IN MIND
How do you want to be remembered?
Define your mission and goals in life.

3 PUT FIRST THINGS FIRST
Prioritize important activities
over urgent activities

4 THINK WIN-WIN
Create mutually beneficial solutions
in your relationships

**5 SEEK FIRST TO UNDERSTAND,
THEN TO BE UNDERSTOOD**
Use empathic listening to create a caring,
problem-solving atmosphere

6 SYNERGIZE
Combine your s trengths to achieve goals
that can't be reached individually

7 SHARPEN THE SAW
Continuous self-renewal
and self-improvement

Illustration 1.1. 7 Habits of Highly Effective People

Sharpening the Saw means preserving and enhancing the greatest asset you have—you. It means having a balanced program for self-renewal in the four areas of your life: physical, social/emotional, mental, and spiritual. As you renew yourself in each of these four areas, you will begin to focus on your mind, body, heart, and soul to create growth and change in your life.

Renew Yourself

PHYSICAL

- Stay active
- Eat nourishing foods
- Rest and recharge
- Care for your health

MENTAL

- Read and explore new ideas
- Keep learning
- Write and reflect
- Practice problem-solving

EMOTIONAL

- Build strong relationships
- Show kindness and empathy
- Laugh and share joy
- Support others

SPIRITUAL

- Meditate or reflect
- Keep a journal
- Connect with meaning or purpose
- Embrace uplifting experiences

Illustration 1.2. Sharpen the Saw

Wheel of Life

We believe in an approach beyond the four areas that Covey describes, which is how the *Wheel of Life* can be used to constantly assess multiple areas of our life. *The Wheel of Life* plays a role in who you put on your board.

But what is the *Wheel of Life* and how do we use it when it comes to building our board? What are the categories? When you Google *Wheel of Life* you find many variations, but most of the categories are very similar. These are the categories we have chosen. We have added a *Growth Mindset* category to our *Wheel of Life* because we think it is so important.

1. Fun
2. Finance
3. Friends and Family
4. Growth Mindset
5. Personal and Professional Growth
6. Relationships
7. Spirituality
8. Wellbeing

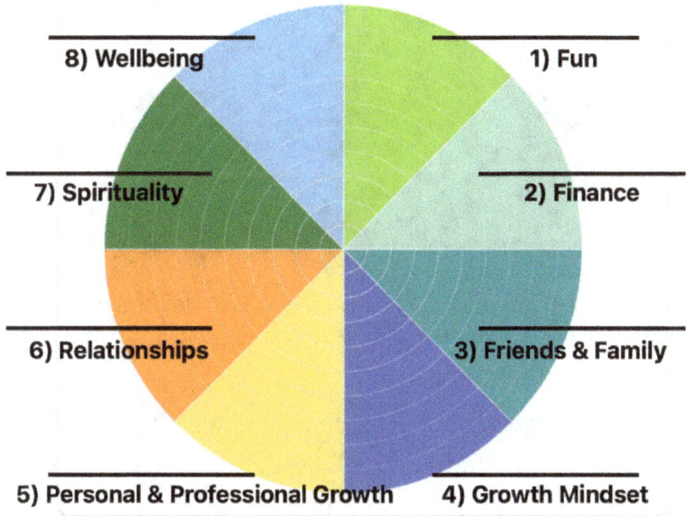

Illustration 1.3. Wheel of Life

The *Wheel of Life* provides categories for reflection to bring balance to your life and create happiness and success. It originates from Tibetan Buddhism and focuses on eight components, which are also called happiness factors in human life. The *Wheel of Life* is one of the most common subjects of Buddhist art. The detailed symbolism of the *Wheel* can be interpreted on many levels. The *Wheel of Life* (called the Bhavachakra in Sanskrit) represents the cycle of birth and rebirth and existence in samsara.

Illustration 1.4. The Bhavachakra is a Tibetan Buddhist representation of the "wheel of life," or cycle of existence. Maren Yumi / Flickr

The *Wheel of Life* first emerged as a personal development tool in the Western world in the 1960s and 1970s. Paul J. Meyer, the founder of Success Motivation Institute and a pioneer in the self-improvement industry, developed it. However, this method should not be confused with the Tibetan version, which focuses more on the awareness of the personal state of mind.

The *Wheel of Life* is a simple but powerful tool that provides a 360° view of all the important areas of your life at once. It is often used by life coaches and career coaches to give their clients a bird's-eye view of their lives. It quickly identifies areas of imbalance and helps you to create goals and set priorities based on your life vision.

What makes your heart sing? What gets you bouncing out of bed in the morning? What gives you energy? What are you working towards? Twenty-five years ago in his book *The 7 Habits of Highly Effective People,* Stephen Covey told us to work "with the end in mind," and his message to begin each day, task, or project with a clear vision of your desired destination is as powerful today as it was then.

The wheel helps you to better understand which of your life areas are flourishing and which ones need the most work by looking at a visual representation of all the areas of your life at once.. Without the wheel, you wouldn't know where to begin when it comes to building your dream (personal) board of directors. Of course, you may know you want a promotion or to go to the gym more often, but our *Wheel of Life* approach will have you diving much deeper into what truly brings you joy.

The best part of all? This can enable you to live a life maximizing your full potential.

How an Alleged Pyramid Scheme Became the Entry Way Towards the *Wheel of Life*

I had a paper route when I was twelve. I was in Junior Achievement when I was thirteen. I cleaned rooms at the Beach Cottages (that are still there in Pacific Beach) when I was fifteen. When I was around seventeen years old, a family friend introduced me to Amway. At that time Amway was recognized as a household name for organic cleaning products that were sold through multi-level marketing. I was clearly interested in getting ahead starting at a young age!

Amway believed that "owning a business could help you reach your full potential and provide a better life for you and your family." Despite the fact that Amway "encouraged" books, seminars and rallies resembling religious revival meetings, I walked away with a life-long appreciation for the Silva Method and the power of a positive mindset through Napoleon Hill's, *Think and Grow Rich*.

I was too young to realize that Amway was a pyramid scheme, but I was introduced to two influential authors and ways of thinking—Dale Carnegie's *How to Win Friends and Influence People* and Napoleon Hill's *Think and Grow Rich*. *Think and Grow Rich* was written for salesmen in 1937!

Over the years, I have learned from many of my skillful and successful friends and colleagues that the power of positive thinking is the key to manifesting your intentions, and curating your own board of directors is the secret to mastering this skill! Thoughts are things, so be intentional with your thoughts. One of my own board of directors is my co-author Dr. Leena Guptha. She is one of my board members in what we have included as the Growth Mindset category that we will share more about in chapter five.

—From Stacy

First, we need to clarify the difference between a *traditional* board of directors and your own *personal* board of directors. Chapter one will cover *traditional* corporate thinking of boards, what makes a board great, and *new* thinking for a *personal* board. If you think your career-oriented board of directors is sufficient to help you live your life to the fullest, you may want to continue reading.

Traditional Reasons for a Board of Directors

A traditional board of directors is a governing body that represents the shareholders or owners of a company and is responsible for overseeing its overall direction and performance. The board is typically composed of a group of individuals, known as directors, who are elected or appointed by the shareholders.

The primary role of a traditional board is to provide strategic guidance and make decisions on behalf of the company. This includes setting the company's goals and objectives, approving major policies and initiatives, and ensuring that the company operates in compliance with regulations. The board hires and evaluates the performance of the CEO (Chief Executive Officer) and may be involved in executive compensation and succession planning.

A traditional board of directors is usually composed of individuals who are not involved in day-to-day operational activities, has at least one company insider such as a chief executive officer, along with a majority of outside or independent directors with relevant expertise in the industry, financial wisdom, marketing expertise, networking, fundraising, and strategic planning. They bring diverse expertise and experience to the boardroom, often drawn from various industries or professions, and act in the best interest of the company and its shareholders. Board meetings are typically held each quarter, during which directors discuss important matters, review financial reports, and provide guidance to the management team.

Similar to the way that your personal board will be built, the structure and practices of traditional boards vary depending on the company's size, industry, and legal requirements. In some cases, the board may include representatives from other stakeholders, such as employees or external advisors. Additionally, boards may establish committees, such as an audit committee or compensation committee, to focus on specific areas of oversight and provide more specialized expertise.

New Thinking for Your Personal Board of Directors

So, how might you engage with a personal board of directors?

- Help you to gain greater clarity on what you want out of life.
- Take you to another level of understanding in a particular area of interest.
- Help you to recognize and deal with old, self-sabotaging habits.
- Break down daunting goals into manageable steps.
- Ensure long-term goals remain in sight when your focus expands.
- Help you become better prepared.
- Support and motivate you.
- Help you to develop positive habits.
- Asking you questions that you don't ask yourself.
- Challenge you to new ways of thinking.
- Support your ongoing processes.
- Be a sounding board for new ideas.
- Support you past obstacles.
- Keep you accountable and committed to your goals.
- Help you maintain a growth mindset.
- Celebrate your successes!

Most successful people work hard and only think about a mentor or coach when it comes to their career or finances or when a problem arises and is seemingly beyond their ability to find resolution. What they often miss is adding personal board members who can advise them in areas that are not their areas of strength and can help and help identify areas for growth. At every phase of your career, but also in other areas of your life, you could have a personal board of directors, keeping in mind that its make-up and complexion will change as your life evolves. We have seen many people have "successful" careers, but they may not be so focused on other areas of the *Wheel of Life* and, inevitably, they can become unfulfilled, depressed, or sick.

There are mixed feelings about how many people to have on your board. We believe in complete customization. You can have as many people as you need to fill your gaps. You also might have more than one person in a category. Some may stay longer than others, some may be emotionally invested in you, and some you may not even know.

Yes, that's right! You may not even know some of your board members, and that's ok. We call these people "secret" board members, and we will go over their roles in Chapter Two. Board members are people you seek out when you face key decisions, need information they are experts on, or simply need inspiration or motivation from.

I'm sure you, like us, often turn to Google as one of your expert board members du' jour! You might even use Chat GPT or other AI tools. That works sometimes, but our six-step process can help you understand that strategically curating your board will yield positive results that are unachievable through AI.

When putting together a board, it's important to note that the specifics may vary based on the context and the individual or company involved. Table 1.1 provides a general overview of the key differences between a personal board of directors and a corporate board of directors.

	Personal Board of Directors	**Corporate Board of Directors**
Purpose	Personal development, guidance, and support	Governance, decision-making, and fiscal oversight of a company
Composition	Comprised of trusted mentors, advisors, colleagues, peers, and professionals	Comprised of directors elected or appointed by shareholders for particular areas of corporate need
Responsibilities	Provide guidance, advice, and strategic input on personal and professional matters related to your *Wheel of Life*	Determine corporate strategy, hire and evaluate executives, oversee financial performance, and ensure compliance
Decision-Making Authority	Advisory role, no formal decision-making authority	Have the power to make binding financial and legal decisions on behalf of the company
Accountability	Personal accountability to you	Fiduciary duty to act in the best interest of the company and its shareholders
Legal Obligations	No legal obligations, operates informally	Governed by laws, regulations, and fiduciary duties imposed by corporate governance principles
Meetings	Informal meetings, one-on-one, usually scheduled based on individual needs	Formal meetings, typically scheduled periodically with minutes (e.g., quarterly or annually)

Compensation	Unpaid, based on personal relationships	Typically receive compensation (e.g., fees, equity) for their service
Focus	Personal and/or professional growth of the individual	Maximizing shareholder value and ensuring the success of the company

Table 1.1 Differences of Personal Board and
Corporate Board of Directors

The Wheel in Motion

Let's take a look at how our Wheel of Life approach can be put into practice, starting off with our first interview with a colleague.

Kellie Knight is New York campus director of Pacific College of Health and Science, as well as a single parent and role model to her daughter. She is influenced by wellness and fitness—both mind and body—with a passion for helping others reach their full potential. Kellie is active in her community, helping other women of color to grow and develop their own leadership skills.

Kellie's Interview

"You're successful at leading a healthcare college as well as inspiring others. Share with us your path to leadership and applying the Wheel of Life to creating your personal board of directors."

1. *Who has been the most influential person on your path to leadership?*

    The most influential person on my path to leadership has been Dr. Beau Anderson. She was instrumental in seeing my strengths and talents. She helped me see the broad impact of health and wellness and its importance in preventative medicine, creating a passion for the industry which opened my mind to career possibilities.

2. *Do you consider this person one of your personal board members?*

    Yes, I consider Beau one of my personal board members. She has an approachable leadership style that has been a key component to the management style I aim to cultivate.

3. *How has this person influenced your growth?*

    Beau influenced my growth by gently pushing me onto a wider path and inviting me to the table, and listening intently to my contributions, making sure my voice was heard.

4. *Have you added any board members since using the Wheel of Life?*

    Yes, I have added more members—Stacy Gomes, Laura Hardin, Non-profit president. I do need to add more, however.

5. *In what ways have you considered formalizing a relationship with board members?*

    An official request via email that outlines their knowledge and expertise that you hope to draw on is a good place to begin the relationship. It should include their industry experience and professional skills. This may help you keep your board diverse by seeing what each person has to offer.

6. *How has your self-awareness changed since intentionally curating your board?*

    Creating a personal board has forced me to consider the areas I need to improve or uncertainty, such as what are my long-term personal goals and how do they align with my career. Who in my support system can help me grow? It has made me more aware of moments when I may be unofficially on someone else's board and the importance of thoughtful feedback.

By now, you're probably encouraged (we hope) to create your personal board of directors to live your highest potential. Now that we know what a traditional board entails and how you can begin to think about your personal board, it's time to start brainstorming before going deeper into "secret" board members.

Your Next Steps

Now, it's time for step one in our six-step process of curating your personal board.

Make a list of people you look up to who succeeded in something that impresses you.

1. What did they do that impressed you?
2. Do you know the path they took?
3. Are they alive?
4. Do you or could you talk to them?
5. In what ways might their story help you improve?

Chapter 2

YOUR SECRET BOARD MEMBERS

"Surround yourself with only people who are going to lift you higher."

—Oprah Winfrey

So many experts and so much advice! How do you choose the right board member? If you can't surround yourself with who you want on your board then it's time to get resourceful! Since we usually never bring our personal board of directors together face-to-face, it's not necessary to have all of your board members be people who are alive or who you know.

Sounds odd right? But think about it. We all secretly or openly follow certain public figures, authors, YouTubers, TikTokers, Instagrammers, or podcasters who we think we can learn something from. What draws you to these people? What do they provide that you're trying to get more of?

Chapter 1 introduced you to why we all need a personal board of directors. We looked at a traditional board of directors and new thinking on personal boards, as well as categories for a *"Wheel of Life"* and some methods to check-in. In this chapter, we'll go over the concept of "secret" board members and how you likely *already* have some.

Metaphorically speaking, you can consider the people you follow for advice, support, and guidance as your "secret board members." These individuals might not be officially designated as such, but they play similar roles in your life. They are people you trust, whose opinions you value, and whose insights help you make decisions and navigate various aspects of your life.

These "secret board members" can include mentors, close friends, family members, colleagues, teachers, and anyone else who has a positive and significant impact on your personal and professional growth. They offer diverse perspectives, challenge your thinking, provide emotional support, and contribute to your decision-making process. The question is do we want to keep them as "secret" board members or do we want to reach out and let them know?

> One person I have on my board for health, longevity, and nutrition, whom I've never even met, is Ben Greenfield. Ben has a bachelor's and master's degree in sports science, exercise, and physiology. He is one of my "secret" board members. I follow his Instagram and podcasts, and he has replied to my comments before, but other than that, we have no contact.
>
> Why do I have him on my board? He is an expert on human physiology and anti-aging and keeps up with the latest science and literature that I don't have time to read in areas that help me with daily peak performance.
>
> Another secret board member I have is Jocko Willink. I, however, do know Jocko. I trained cross-fit with him for years at his gym in San Diego. I can tell you that having an ex-Navy SEAL stand next to you yelling, "You got this! … Push harder!" is enough to make you work harder! His leadership books, training, and advice are read and followed by thousands.

Would I tell him he is on my board? Probably not because he's so famous now and he makes a living advising very high-level leaders. I will continue to listen to his podcasts, read his books, be motivated by his words, and learn an immense amount from his leadership experience as a Navy SEAL.

—From Stacy

A secret board member I've never met is Louise Hay. I've never even thought to reach out to her. She serves as my secret board member through her books on positivity, and her resources are much aligned with what I think and how I teach. You could say she is my growth-mindset secret board member.

Another secret board member who I have known for years is Leon Chaitow DO (RIP), who authored over seventy books in osteopathic medicine. He encouraged me to write as well, but as a famous and eminent author (even if living), I'm not sure that I would have asked him to be on my board. However, he continues to live on through my osteopathic teaching.

This is just one of the many powers of secret board members. The value they give you can continue to live on in the work you do for years to come without managing an entire in-person traditional board.

—From Dr. Leena

While they might not be part of a formal board of directors, these individuals collectively influence your journey and contribute to your overall growth. It's essential to nurture and maintain these relationships, as they can provide invaluable guidance and insights throughout your life.

Who Are You Following and Why?

These "secret" experts might provide mini reports, articles, websites, YouTube videos, newsletters, blogs, or recommendations of what to read or pay attention to. What books or articles are they reading? What devices are they using? What influencers are they following? What are they posting? What conferences have they attended? What retreat has inspired them? What art are they loving? What music are they listening to? What causes are they supporting? We sometimes get even more valuable advice from secret board members than the ones we personally know and meet with because there are often fewer limits on what we *can* learn from them. Anything they post is fair game.

Let's consider how a secret board member might work for you:

- They post educational content that helps you level up your skill set.
- They do homework for you.
- They don't judge you because they don't know you.
- They provide inspiration and new insights.
- They can motivate you to try something new with no pressure.
- You won't feel obligated to report to them.
- You can follow them without them knowing, continually getting free insights.

The Role of Secret Board Members

You likely already have individuals that could be categorized as "secret" board members. Good for you! We'll look at what role they play in the next chapter. Selecting secret board members—individuals who inspire and offer confidential guidance and support—requires careful consideration.

Here are 4 steps to help you identify potential secret board members:

1. **Define your needs:** Determine which aspects of your life or business you need guidance on. Are you seeking advice on personal development, career growth, industry insights, or something else?

2. **Identify expertise:** Consider the areas in which you lack expertise or would benefit from diverse perspectives. Look for individuals with relevant experience, knowledge, and insights that can contribute meaningfully. The more specific, the better!

3. **Industry leaders:** Look for individuals who are leaders in your industry or field. They offer insights into trends, challenges, and opportunities that can guide your decisions.

4. **Seek out those with diverse backgrounds:** Seek individuals with diverse backgrounds, experiences, and perspectives. This diversity can bring fresh ideas and approaches to your decision-making process, which is what expanding your traditional board and moving into this approach is all about.

When I talk to people about their *Wheel of Life* and the areas in which they may need a board member, the one that consistently comes up is financial. It is also the category that I consistently rate lower than others on my *Wheel of Life* and look for guidance. After all, I think we all want to "strengthen our finances."

But what does this mean? Our financial position changes over the years, and now when I think about strengthening my finances, I think of being able to retire early with little or no debt! This is where your secret board may come into play. Who plays that role for you? Who or what are you following that can help you reach those goals?

—From Stacy

I use the *Wheel of Life* as an assessment tool in practice. I've found that people resonate with a secret board member in health, which is an area I'm constantly working to improve through an array of secret board members in the public domain.

It raises the question, *What does it mean to be healthy?* For me personally, it also relates to the values question, *What does it mean to be happy?* When I think of health, I think of the mind, body, and spirit balance, and that equates to my daily happiness. This is where I seek out secret board members who can support whole health and wellbeing, whether through a blog, a social media post, or a conference. Who plays that role for you? Who inspires your health and wellbeing?

—From Dr. Leena

We could all use financial advisors on our board, but many of us do not know these types of experts, and most financial advisors have different strategies. One of our friends stated she knows financial advisors but wouldn't be comfortable asking them to be a board member since they charge for this service.

So, we pivoted the mindset and had a conversation about what she brought to the table for them! Not everyone wants to be paid, it can often just be an exchange of value. Many people have social capital or a wide network to draw on that is equally attractive. Focusing on your end game will help you pick who plays this role for you.

But who do you add to your board and how do you pick?

Dead or Alive

We sometimes lean on famous or successful deceased people like Leon Chaitow, DO. We also follow LinkedIn, Instagram, and podcasts.

A famous person, even if you'll never meet them in person, can still play a valuable role as a "virtual" secret board member by offering insights, inspiration, and guidance through their public statements, writings, and actions. Even though a secret board member is deceased and cannot actively participate in discussions, their insightful advice from books, investments, teachings, or art can still contribute significantly to your personal growth and decision-making process.

Yes, Famous and Deceased Experts Can Be on Your Board.

Here's how:

Guidance Through Literature: Draw upon the writings, books, or teachings of the deceased secret board member as a source of timeless wisdom. Their insights can serve as a foundation for your decision-making and problem-solving. You're likely already doing this! Considering these thought leaders as official "secret board members" will help you organize your learning processes and stay consistent.

Strategic Planning: As such, the wisdom left behind by the deceased secret board member can be integrated into your long-term strategic planning. Their philosophies and principles can shape your overarching goals and direction. This is why it's beneficial to consider them *official* members of your board—you can continually gain insights from them and implement these insights accordingly.

Inspiration: Famous individuals often have stories of resilience, innovation, and success that can inspire you to overcome challenges and pursue your goals. Quotes, anecdotes, and teachings from a deceased secret board member can inspire innovative thinking and creative solutions to challenges you're facing. If we aren't inspired by our board, what are we doing?

Moral and Ethical Framework: Use their ethical and moral principles as a guide when making decisions that require ethical considerations. This ensures that you're aligning your choices with their values. Study the values and principles demonstrated by the famous person's actions and decisions. You can apply these to your own decision-making process and ethical considerations.

Mentorship from Afar: Treat famous or deceased public statements and interviews as a form of mentorship from a distance. Treat their writings as a form of mentorship from beyond the grave. You can learn from their experiences and apply their lessons to your own journey.

Legacy Lessons: Famous individuals often leave behind legacies that offer valuable lessons. Analyze their legacy and consider how you can create a meaningful impact in your own endeavors. Someone who has played a legacy role for me is Napoleon Hill, author of *Think and Grow Rich*. His wise lessons about the power of the mind have stuck with me since I was given the book at age seventeen. By integrating the teachings of the deceased into your decision-making, you're preserving and honoring their legacy, ensuring that their wisdom continues to influence and guide others.

Advisory Framework: Create a written record of how you believe the deceased secret board member's advice would apply to various situations. This becomes a resource you can consult when faced with challenges.

Sharing Insights: If appropriate, share the insights from the deceased secret board member with your trusted mentors, advisors, or confidantes. Their perspectives could provide additional clarity and make your board feel more official and comprehensive, which is what this is all about!

Personal Branding: If the famous person's brand or image aligns with your goals, you can learn from their strategies for building and maintaining a strong personal brand. This is especially useful with secret board members since you'll likely primarily be keeping up with them online! Whether or not they post branding content may not matter in some situations, because you'll have access to their entire online brand either way, which can help you draw inspiration and gain insights when it comes to your own marketing.

Expanding Perspectives: The famous person's perspective can broaden your own worldview and help you consider alternative viewpoints, especially if their expertise is broader than yours at the moment. It's all about seeing things from a different filter, not just a mirror that reflects back what you already know. Often, the famous and deceased are well-known for their unique or extra-specific ways of working and teaching. This makes them distinctly helpful for broadening your own perspective and putting these insights to use.

It's important to approach this secret relationship with a balance between admiration and critical thinking. While the insights of a famous or deceased person can be valuable, remember that every individual's journey is unique. Ultimately, the role of a famous person as a virtual secret board member is to provide you with additional perspectives, insights, and inspiration that can help you make informed decisions and achieve your goals.

By incorporating their insights into your decision-making process and not merely reading their work without applying it, you're benefiting from their perspective and honoring their contributions to your personal growth and development. Putting what you've learned to use is what having a *useful* board is all about.

Chapter 1 introduced why strategically creating a personal board of directors is so effective for manifesting a fulfilling life as well as the difference between a traditional board and a personal board of directors. In this chapter, we spoke about secret board members and how to tap into their expertise. In the next chapter, you will learn how to start curating your own board using our *Wheel of Life* approach.

The Wheel in Motion

Elizabeth (Liza) Goldblatt, PhD, MHA/PA has been involved in healthcare education for over 30 years, including working with mainstream/conventional medical providers and the complementary and integrated healthcare providers in collaborative research, educational, and clinical settings. She served as the Executive Director of the Academic Collaborative for Integrative Health, the president of the Council of Colleges of Acupuncture and Herbal Medicine, and sat on the Board of Trustees for Pacific University. From 1988-2003, Goldblatt was president of the Oregon College of Oriental Medicine and Provost and Vice President of Academic Affairs at the American College of Traditional Chinese Medicine. She currently serves on the National Academy of Medicine's Global Forum for Global Innovations in Health Professional Education.

Interview with Elizabeth Goldblatt, PhD:

1. *Who do you consider secret board members at the moment?*

   I have nine secret board members for different aspects of my life:

   I have three board members for input on my professional work who are long-time colleagues. I have three-plus board members for my questions about health and wellbeing. And, I have three board members for general advice on my life.

2. *Why did you pick these people?*

   My "work" board members are direct, have significant expertise and experience, are kind and supportive, and I have deep respect for them. My "health and wellbeing" board members are long-time health professionals with very broad expertise and experience. They know me and my history well and communicate with one another. My three board members for general life advice are long-time friends, and I trust them implicitly. They are also very honest, direct, blunt, and caring—we relax together, hike together, and play together.

All my board members and I share core life values and can communicate with each other at deep meaningful levels. We are direct, blunt, kind, and compassionate with one another. Being a dearth of compassion these days, I strongly believe that kindness is essential for wellbeing.

In addition, while not being a board member, I am very fortunate to have many contacts in my work life—depending on what kind of knowledge and skills I need to access. These colleagues are more like having a large Advisory Board. While I have three main individuals who are my health and wellness professionals and good friends, I am also able to access many others if needed. At any age, we all need "board members" who are both kind and caring as well as direct, honest, very smart, and who one deeply respects.

3. *How have they added to your growth so far?*

    We are not on this planet alone. We all need community, we all need a variety of "board members" and we all need to keep learning—intellectually, emotionally, and spiritually. At a very young age, I made a commitment to become self-aware, to know myself, my strengths, areas to improve, personal triggers, etc. I became spiritually committed to meditation and decided it was important to do professional work that benefits others.

    Our environment, who we know, who we choose to be with, and where we spend our time all offer the opportunity for growth. Each of my Board members has added to my growth, as we are all interconnected. And we chose our board members for their wisdom, caring, and commitment to build a better, saner planet. All my Board members have similar core life values.

As long as we are on this planet, we have the opportunity to grow and learn and be of benefit to others. Depending on where we are in our age and professional work, we need different board members. I know that for me now, I need ones who are both direct and smart, as well as caring and kind.

In writing this, I also realized a while ago that my three main spiritual teachers have passed and that created a significant gap for me. While not being a formal Secret Board Member, I also have a Curandero/Marriage Family Therapist with whom I consult when needed. I tell him he is a "spiritual teacher" in MFT clothing.

All my board members have added to my growth in so many ways, as we can always grow professionally, personally, emotionally, and spiritually. This is a life-long path. Thus, having board members in each of these four areas is most helpful as we walk on this most interesting path of life.

Your Next Steps

Next, identify a few more secret board members who can help you improve, and ask yourself:

1. What are the top three questions you would ask each of them?
2. How would you act if you were in the room with them?
3. What could they expect from you?

HOW TO CURATE YOUR BOARD
USING THE *WHEEL OF LIFE*

*"Great board members are not just experts in their fields,
but individuals who possess the wisdom to make tough decisions,
the courage to challenge the status quo, and the vision to guide
the organization (you) towards success."*

—Unknown

In Chapter 1, we learned why a personal board of directors is effective for manifesting a fulfilling life as well as the difference between a traditional and personal board of directors. Chapter 2 provided ideas on secret board members and how to use them. In this chapter, you will learn how to curate your board using our *Wheel of Life* approach.

The ocean of uncertainty is ever-present in all of our lives no matter who we are. This ocean is deep and wide, which is why we need people to help us navigate the unknown waters that we can't predict. In doing so, we typically turn to our friends, family, and loved ones. But what if you had your own board of directors as well? Imagine having a perfectly curated, personal board by your side whenever you need the right information at the right time.

Creating your personal board with our *Wheel of Life* approach will give you all you need at hand whenever you need a boost—any type of boost! Whether it's professional guidance from someone you admire or personal advice from a loved one, think about what role everyone could potentially play.

> When I was doing my master's degree at San Diego State University, I wanted to learn how to write grants. Writing grants is not an easy process. I was interested in this skill knowing it would help my career as a researcher. But where do you start? Back then, there weren't Google "how-to" guides or AI apps to help so it was sheer grunt work in the library and old-funded grants!
>
> I stumbled along with various baby grants in the College of Education, making mistakes, until I was able to find a mentor in the College of Sciences. I was referred to Dr. Kathleen M. Fisher. Dr. Fisher is Professor Emeritus of Biology at San Diego State University and former Director of the Center for Research in Mathematics and Science Education where I ended up working for five years.
>
> She was a well-established researcher with the National Science Foundation and generously took me under her wing. Knowing that grant writing was a skill I wanted to acquire to advance my academic career, I jumped right in and soaked up all the advice I received from Dr. Fisher.
>
> Dr. Fisher was patient and committed to having me involved with every aspect of writing a grant, implementing the work, tracking the progress, writing up the findings, submitting to journals, and presenting at the American Association for the Advancement of Science. Looking back, I had no idea that she was really the first member of my board of directors.

She encouraged me to get a doctoral degree and to visualize myself with other researchers and academic leaders teaching, writing, and helping others understand how science improves our lives. I would put this in the professional growth category of my *Wheel of Life* and you will see how we pick and choose what area to focus on later on.

—From Stacy

Mentor, Coach, or Board Member?

Having a personal board member is different than having a mentor or coach. Many people mistakenly think these are the same. Mentors typically serve as a source of guidance and wisdom and coaches use their skills and techniques to enable the client to define goals and identify measures of success. Board members are more long-term strategic thinkers, and they are meant to work *for you!*

We have both mentored hundreds (if not thousands) of students and faculty combined over the years and set up mentoring programs and structures for them along the way. The limitation with a mentor can be that the relationship is usually informal and voluntary with limited accountability.

I have had personal coaches/trainers most of my life with bodybuilding, running, swimming, triathlons, Muay Thai martial arts, and now moving into strength and mobility work. This relationship dynamic is a paid formal agreement to provide specific skills, techniques, and strategies focused on outcomes. Usually, we hold our coaches accountable to keep us on track and they hold us accountable to help us reach our goals.

—From Stacy

I've had a business coach for many years who has a corporate background. He has introduced me to other clients he mentors and expanded my worldview of finance and business. He has a corporate way of saying what I need to hear to move me forward (it's not always what I want to hear). Our contractual agreement differentiates the relationship from my personal board members.

—From Dr. Leena

Board members usually serve a long-term commitment. They are accountable to the stakeholders (you) and usually provide specific expertise.

As a board member, I have served on five different boards and have reported to two. This service provides me the unique opportunity to see how a board member can move an organization forward and the various expertise required for specific needs. Some board members can be very active and involved (sometimes too much) and others are more passive and wait to be asked for an opinion or task.

—From Stacy

I've served on several health-focused boards in various capacities. In fact, I met co-author Dr. Stacy Gomes through serving on a board. Through the years, she has been my mentor in academic affairs, my coach as my formal supervisor, and today, serves as my wellbeing personal board member on my board of directors.

—From Dr. Leena

Let's look at a quick comparison between the roles of mentor, coach, and board member.

Aspect	Mentor	Coach	Corporate Board Member
1) Role	Offers guidance, wisdom, and advice based on personal experience	Provides support, evokes awareness and accountability to help individuals or groups reach goals	Governs and advises an organization strategically
2) Focus	Personal and professional development	Individual growth and development	Organizational development
3) Relationship Dynamics	Informal and voluntary	Can be formal or informal, paid or unpaid	Formal and contractual
4) Expertise	Offers specific knowledge and experience in a specific field or industry	Utilizes coaching skills, techniques, and strategies in specific areas of the formal coaching agreement	Brings expertise in a specific field or industry
5) Duration	Can be short-term or long-term	Can be short-term or long-term	Usually long-term commitment
6) Accountability	Generally, less structured	Focused on achieving identified measures of success	Accountable to stakeholders

Table 3.1 Comparison of Mentor, Coach, and Board Member

How to Be Strategic While Picking Your People

There are two ways you can pick your board members:

1. Make a list of all the cool, smart people you know and just pick their brains!

   Or...

2. Identify the areas you want to strengthen using the *Wheel of Life*. (5 out of 5 stars for sure! Highly recommend!)

Before you start randomly picking board members from your list of exceptional and impressive friends and colleagues, you need to identify the areas that you want to strengthen and need expertise in. When your board is aligned with a clear focus on the areas you want to strengthen you will grow in so many unexpected ways. The more specific you can get, the better! We'll go deeper into this at the end of the chapter so that you'll leave with extra clarity on how to build the perfect board.

Categories of My Life Book

I've kept a "Life Book" for about fifteen years. This book consisted of ten categories that guided me towards people and information to focus on various areas of my life. They haven't changed much over the years, and almost every area I want to improve fits into one of these categories.

1. Health/wellness
2. Fitness
3. Nutrition
4. Knowledge and learning
5. Consciousness (spiritual, emotional, character)
6. Love and relationships

7. Career, business, success

8. Travel, social, friends

9. Wealth and prosperity

10. Family

My Life Book was in a three-ring binder years ago. Yeah… Remember those?! I know that seems ancient and old-fashioned, but I liked it because I would keep lists and sometimes photos, articles, or mementos to remind me of areas of interest and encourage my focus. Most of the pictures were on travel and fitness, so back then it felt a little visually lopsided!

I moved it to a digital Word document, although it no longer adds the fun visual elements. The benefit of the digital file is that I now compare different years, goals, and accomplishments. Instead of stressing myself out about New Year's resolutions, I reflect on the areas of my *Wheel of Life* periodically to see if I've moved the needle or need to refocus my attention and support. The great advantage of using our *Wheel of Life* is you can update it periodically and see where your changes are since it saves your last entry!

—From Stacy

Stacy's *Wheel of Life*:

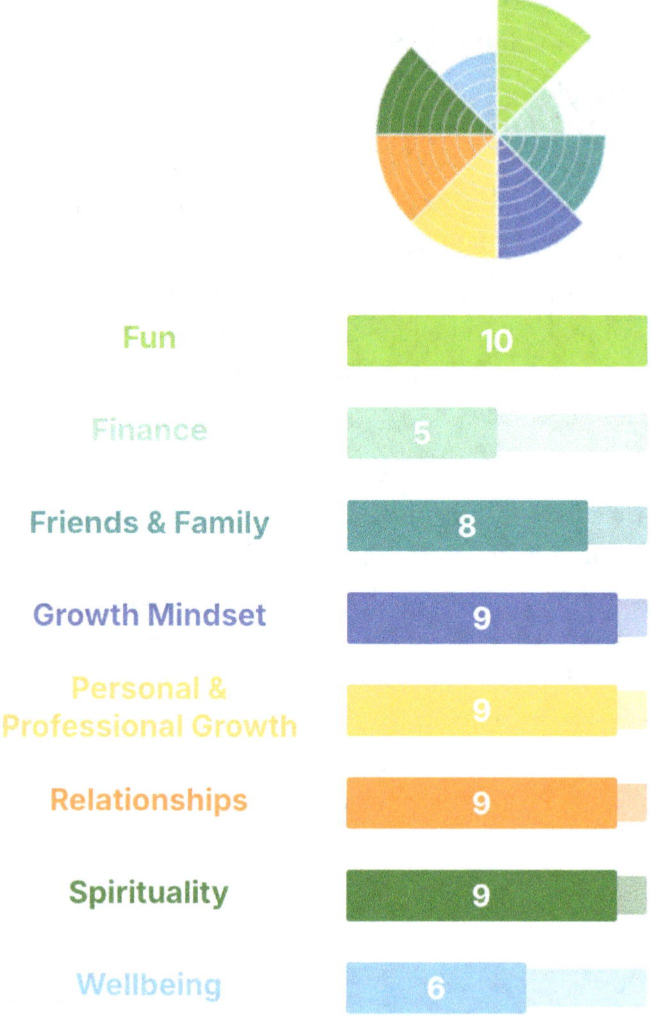

Figure 3.1 Stacy's Wheel of Life

You can see that I rated the "Finance" category a five and the "Wellbeing" category a six. The reason I rated "Finance" a six is that I want to eliminate all debt to achieve financial freedom.

My goal is to pay off debt to retire more comfortably. I mean, don't we all want that! I don't know if anyone is a ten in "Finance." (If you're out there, I want you on my board!) I am adding board members in this area and have been a member of Dow Jane for about a year now.

I recently wanted to explore more visual cues for the areas of the *Wheel of Life* around "Finance." I looked at my Pinterest account to see if any of these categories are represented. Wow! I was super surprised! Most of my boards were about beautiful backyards, all things tiki, vintage, great-looking recipes, jewelry, and floral design! What?! No career or wealth inspo?!

I started looking at new boards using the keywords in the other categories with the intention of being more visual and strategic using the *Wheel of Life*. I was happy to find most of the areas of the *Wheel of Life* represented and have added two new categories to my Pinterest: "Professional Growth" and "Wealth and Prosperity." That's a fun exercise for you if you are a creative visual person who uses Pinterest!

Figure 3.2. Pinterest "Wealth and Prosperity"

Leena's *Wheel of Life*:

I use the *wheel of life* in practice as an assessment tool and to monitor myself.

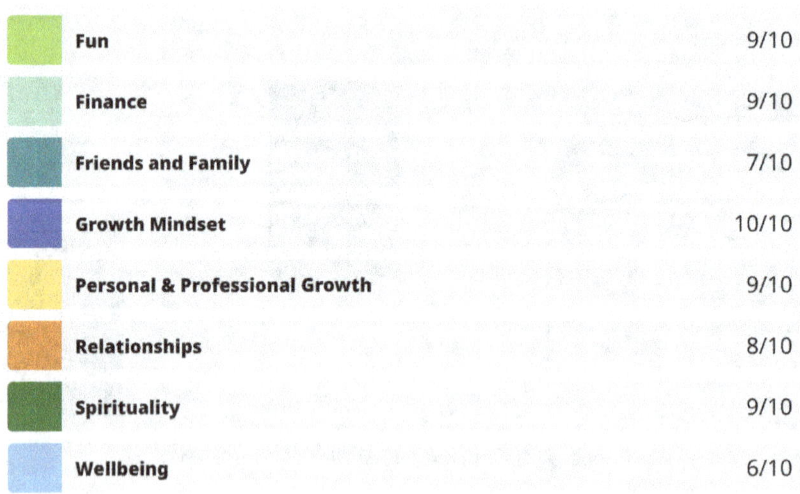

Figure 3.3 Leena's Wheel of Life

You can see that I rated the "Wellbeing" category a six (lower than other areas) because, though I sleep like a log, rest well, and all of the medical labs I could think to test recently (except HbA1c) are within normal limits (so technically I'm in great shape for a senior), regular exercise has always been my greatest challenge.

Also related to the wellbeing category is nutrition. When I eat well, I eat lots of vegetables, and well-balanced and organic food but other times I'm quite the "snacker." My nutrition varies with my environment. These two together relate to wellbeing and health, and as my mother would say, "Health is wealth!"

Figure 3.4. Pinterest "Exercise"

Wheel of Life

This wheel contains eight sections that, together, represent one way of describing a whole life.

1. Fun
2. Friends and Family
3. Finance
4. Growth Mindset
5. Personal and Professional Growth

6. Relationships

7. Spirituality

8. Wellbeing

You may have other labels or categories or may wish to divide them into categories such as career, nutrition, exercise, teamwork, etc. The structure is entirely up to you. The exercise measures your level of satisfaction in these areas on the day you work through this exercise. It is not a picture of how it has been in the past or what you want it to be in the future. It is a snapshot taken at the moment. It is not a report card on how well you performed or what you have achieved. The emphasis is your level of satisfaction in each area.

The *Wheel of Life* provides a unique model. The wheel shows what balance in your life looks like. This can be used to identify which areas you may choose to add a board member. Once you have completed the *Wheel of Life* exercise, you will have a clear sense of the areas you may wish to focus on.

Composing a personal board of directors can be a great way to gain guidance and support in achieving your goals. Here are some steps you can take to create your own personal board of directors:

1. Define your goal areas using the *Wheel of Life*: Take some time to think about your personal and professional goals and what type of guidance or support you need to achieve them. For example, you may need help with personal or professional development, financial planning, wellbeing, or growth mindset.

2. Identify potential board members: Think about people in your network who have the skills, expertise, and experience to help you achieve your goals. They could be colleagues, mentors, friends, or family members. Just as Stacy connected

with the right expert to help her write grants, it's always best to aim for the specific guidance you need.

3. Branch out to even more board members: Yes, once you have your potential board, consider broadening the scope even more. Whether it's someone who has expertise you don't, someone in an industry you've dreamed about entering, or someone of a different generation than you, take a moment to look at your current board and brainstorm what can be added. How can you leave your comfort zone to reach your goals, and who will be needed? It's been said that you should always be surrounded by those smarter than you in the area you want to excel in, and your board is no exception. In fact, a recent report from the Center for Creative Leadership indicates that diversity of behavior brought about by various age groups will be crucial for any board hoping to tackle future-focused issues like sustainability and technology. In any case, your board needs forward thinkers!

4. Make a list: Once you have identified all potential board members, make a list of their names and contact information.

5. Reach out to them: Contact each person on your list, and explain your goals and the purpose of your personal board of directors. Ask them if they would be willing to serve as a member of your board.

6. Schedule a meeting: Once you have identified your board members, schedule a meeting to introduce them to each other and discuss your goals and needs. You may also want to set up regular meetings or check-ins to assess if everyone is on the same page.

7. Set expectations: Be clear about your expectations for each board member and what you hope to achieve from your

board. You may want to set specific goals and timelines for your personal development.

8. Follow up and show appreciation: Stay in touch with your board members and show appreciation for their time and support. Update them on your progress and let them know how their guidance has helped you.

Most people will be flattered by your request and will enjoy the opportunity to guide you. If they don't have the interest, they will let you know. Let everyone know that it's an informal process, and you'll be in touch by phone, e-mail, or even text.

As you utilize your board to help you work toward your goals, continually daydream about your vision. This is a tried, and true method for success. Athletes regularly use the power of visualization to push themselves through the hardest times by visualizing crossing the finish line first, feeling the elation of winning, hearing the cheers, seeing the crowds, and holding the trophy or medal. Don't just daydream without any intent—set the intention to make your daydream a reality in the near future!

After completing the *Wheel of Life*, you can see what is working well and what you might want to focus on. You know what you want, and you have the steps for change towards your vision. Getting the right board members will help you get there.

Allow yourself to be guided by the desired future and goals you choose to daydream about. Visualization and the growth mindset is a powerful first step to getting what you want. Take the *Wheel of Life* challenge with this in mind. Use it to focus on what is going on in all areas of your life and compare this to what you really want to see happening. Notice where the imbalance lies, visualize your ideal future, recognize areas for development, and do what you need to do to bring yourself closer to your goal with the help of your board members.

To put it simply, your personal board can help close the gap between where you're at and where you want to be.

The Wheel in Motion

Dr. Erin Raskin is the Director of inpatient Integrative Medicine at UCSD Center for Integrative Medicine

1. *Were you surprised at your results after you completed the Wheel of Life?*

   Not necessarily surprising, and I liked seeing the topics and having to contemplate how much attention and intention each area is receiving vs. needing. And it certainly changes along the path.

2. *In what way did the results of the Wheel of Life change how you think about seeking support?*

   It has me thinking how to prioritize it all, and where I want to ask for support

3. *What areas of the Wheel of Life have you added personal board members to and why?*

   This will now have to be determined and looking forward to pondering this more!

Your Next Steps

Complete the "*Wheel of Life*" and identify the three categories you want to focus on.

whosonyourboardwheeloflife.com

Once this is complete, review your *Wheel of Life* using the questions below:

- What surprised you?
- Which areas are higher than you thought?
- Which areas are lower than you thought?
- Does this line up with what you value?
- Which areas are most important to you?
- How can you make changes to improve those areas?
- What changes can you make in the next three months in two of those areas?
- Who can you share your commitment with?

Understanding Your Scores

8 – 10: If you have scored 8 – 10 for any of the categories, it means you are very satisfied in this particular area. It is important to ensure that this is maintained, and to keep in mind that improvement in this area is always possible.

5 – 7: If you have scored 5 – 7 for any of the categories, you are reasonably satisfied in that particular area, but you can explore opportunities to move further in this category.

0 – 4: If you have scored 0 – 4 for any of the categories, you are not very satisfied in this particular area, and you may want to explore ways of enhancing your satisfaction here. This is in fact very exciting because you haven't explored fully the opportunities that are available to you in this area.

When choosing your three priority areas, you can choose a high category that you want to improve in even further. For example, Leena would like to see her personal and professional development at a 10, but you can choose to focus goals on lower areas. Stacy wanted to get her finance category to a 9. Your top three priority areas are those most important to you.

HOW YOUR BOARD MEMBERS CAN WORK WITH YOU

*"Your success is contingent on your board doing their best
to help you—so put them to work."*

—Jeff Bonforte

"When I was a young entrepreneur, board meetings
were by far the worst days of my life.

Once I realized the board was there to help and
not just to judge, I became much better at asking for
and getting that help." (The Secret to Making Board
Meetings Suck Less)

OK! You've completed the *Wheel of Life,* and you see the areas
that you may want to work on. What's your next step? Your
next step is getting the right people on your bus.

How do you find the people you'd dream of having on your board?
Who are they?
How can they end up serving you?

If you're like most people, you will ask a friend or Google it, or nowadays, possibly use Chat GPT and other AI tools. But what matters even more than the individuals or information you add to your board is *how* you leverage them. Think: *How can you use these new additions to balance out your Wheel of Life? How does adding each board member positively impact a particular area of your life? Are you comfortable reaching out to these people? How will you present your area of need? What do you bring to the table that they can benefit from?*

Chapter 4 will show you how your board members can work with you based on your *Wheel of Life* categories. You don't need to have board meetings, and IF you do, they don't have to be at the lowest times of your life. It's universally agreed that board meetings are boring! This entire book exists to flip that script!

First, you *are* the organization, and each area of your *Wheel of Life* represents a "project" your board members want to hear about and see how they can contribute. There is no need to hold boring in-person board meetings. Each member should serve on your board for a specific reason. Make sure you're fully tapping into their networks and special skills. That means one-on-one time with each and some more than others. Some of my board members I only talk to once or twice a year, or there can even be years in between when I need them. For example, in times of transition, they are there.

> One of my board members is Dr. Leena, and we speak weekly. She is a role model for positivity and a growth mindset. No matter what scenario I am facing, she can find the growth opportunities and flip the script for me! We specifically added this category to our *Wheel of Life* because we both believe having a board member for growth mindset is crucial to all the other categories.

Another board member I've had for over twenty years is Liza Goldblatt. She has been a wise colleague and friend, keeping me informed about areas of need in medical and healthcare education with the National Academy of Medicine and several other organizations. She has gently pulled me into national positions of leadership that have been incredibly beneficial to my career and growth. Sometimes we wouldn't pursue these sorts of opportunities without the strong encouragement of these types of board members. We sometimes only speak a couple times a year and other times more frequently as needed.

—From Stacy

I have a board member I've known for over twenty years who has been the President of various colleges, and each time we interact he seems to have the perfect thought-provoking comment or discussion to provide me insight into key decisions. When I had two potential roles emerging, he called the one he thought would be most beneficial to the organization and myself his "Plan A." At a later time, as the interview process unfolded on both fronts, he said, "Let's stay focused on Plan A." He not only kept me on the path but later when I accepted Plan A, helped pave the way for me to quickly become part of the new company.

In a short space of time, there was much change geographically and culturally, collaborating with a new team and managing a new home life and community schedule. This board member became instrumental in my decision-making for the best-fit role and enabled me to see how my strengths could impactfully serve others.

—From Dr. Leena

A personal board of directors can help redefine "You" Version 2.0 and make sure that your growth is sustainable. For a typical board meeting, we compile comprehensive materials, data, and updates in a packet and distribute them to board members at least a week beforehand.

The purpose of your board meetings should never be just to "report out" to board members. It should include specific, actionable goals. This is why these meetings should never be boring—they're always getting you one step closer to some meaningful goal! One of your goals will be to update the board members and provide information, but that's only one. Think of your board meetings as an outlet for having discussions, making decisions, and moving forward on specific projects.

Include a feel-good element that reinforces your mission or a "mission moment" as a part of each meeting. Each meeting should have a component where board members are reminded why they serve on your board. It could be a live testimonial, a letter from a client, feedback from family or friends, etc. Whatever story is shared should be so moving that board members are talking about it with each other, at work, and at home for a week or more!

> Another one of my board members is a businessman, who at times I've met with every week for many months. There were also gaps of months or years. I was so delighted when I took all that I had learned from him over a decade ago, as well as recent offerings and applied the tenets and principles we discussed in reality. He and one other board member not only collectively celebrated with me, but that process of refining and their ongoing joy for me is still a topic for discussion and celebration today.
>
> —From Dr. Leena

Write up an entertaining board member job description and provide it to potential board members during the recruitment process. A good board member job description should also include your expectations.

The Millennial Mandate: Why Diversity Is a Strategic Advantage for Your Board

Nobody wants to be irrelevant. Millennials, Gen Z, and soon Gen Alpha help us to stay relevant. Marco Bizzarri, Gucci's chief executive attributes the fashion company's recent turnaround and growth to a shadow committee made up exclusively of millennials. In the process of building your board, ask yourself, *Do I need a shadow committee?*

Millennials make up the largest generation coming of age, are lucrative consumers, are impacting the workforce, and scaling the corporate ladder. As the first digitally native generation, there's no doubt that on-demand technology and instant access to information have changed the way millennials interact, gain, and share knowledge. Millennials influence lifestyle trends and sway the way companies operate, especially regarding product development, marketing, environmental, and sustainable cause marketing.

As the most educated generation, millennials use their knowledge to create long-term value for stakeholders and consumers. Business isn't just about the bottom line for millennials but taking accountability for actions and ultimately making the world we live in a better place. (https://www.govenda.com/blog/millennials-in-the-boardroom)

But how *can* you leverage board members from a wide range of backgrounds and age groups to reach your goals?

How Shadow Boards Bridge Generational Divides

According to <u>BoardSource</u>, 57% of nonprofit board members are over the age of fifty, while only 17% are under forty. The fresh perspective of younger board members reinvigorates older board members and energizes them to engage with new ideas, emerging technologies, and the increasingly important role of social networks. In what categories of your *Wheel of Life* might you consider adding a younger board member? How might you work with them to help your growth? This is precisely the kind of value-add nonprofits should seek out in board members (Connell, Erin).

In Bonforte's own words:

"After having his own ass handed to him a few times, Bonforte knew things had to change. 'I kept asking other CEOs, How do you do your board meetings? I know I might sound like an idiot, but how do you make these things less miserable? Finally, I ran into a couple guys with some wild ideas. One of them was Mike Maples from Floodgate, who told Bonforte that there are really only four things a board needs to consider:

1. *Has the market (you) changed since we last met? If so, did it affect us negatively or positively?*

2. *Has the team (board/circle) changed? For better or worse?*

3. *Has your position in the market (world/life) changed?*

4. *Did you do what you said you would?*

"Then Dan Rosenweig, CEO of online textbook startup Chegg, chipped in some revolutionary advice. 'He's the one that taught me how to keep boards artificially small, and that it wasn't out of line to give board members action items,' Bonforte says.

"Suddenly, board meetings were no longer about judgment. They were about being productive. *'If you think of your board members as working* *for you, there's no reason to lie or fudge things to look a certain way or prove your competence,' he says. 'If you do those things, your board can't help you effectively.'"*

Your personal board of directors can work for you in a variety of ways, depending on your goals and needs. Below is a comparison of how your mentors, coaches, and board members can support you. As you read through, brainstorm or jot down which of your members could fill which role(s)!

1. Mentorship: A board member with more experience and expertise in your field can provide guidance and wisdom on how to navigate your career or personal development.

2. Networking: A board member with a large network of contacts can help you make valuable connections and open doors for you.

3. Accountability: Board members can help keep you accountable to your goals and provide motivation and support along the way.

4. Financial guidance: A board member with expertise in finance can help you with budgeting, investment, or financial planning.

5. Emotional Support: Board members can be a source of emotional support and encouragement during challenging times.

6. Skill development: Board members can provide opportunities for you to develop new skills or gain new experiences that will help you achieve your goals.

The composition of your personal board of directors will vary based on your needs, goals, and areas of focus. It's essential to choose individuals who complement your strengths and provide diverse perspectives.

Consider the following areas to start building a board with various members who all play valuable roles:

1. Define your needs: Determine what specific areas or aspects of your *Wheel of Life* you need guidance or support on. Are you seeking advice on personal development, career growth, industry insights, or something else? Clarify your objectives.

2. Identify expertise: Consider the areas in which you lack expertise or would benefit from diverse perspectives. Look for individuals with relevant experience, knowledge, and insights who can meaningfully contribute.

3. Trust and Confidentiality: Choose people you trust implicitly and who can maintain confidentiality. Given that these individuals will operate in a confidential capacity, trustworthiness is paramount.

4. Network and Connections: Reach out to your existing network. Friends, colleagues, acquaintances, or mentors might be willing to take on this role. Alternatively, ask your current mentors or advisors if they know anyone who could fill this role.

5. Industry Leaders: Look for individuals who are leaders in your industry or field. They can offer insights into industry trends, challenges, and opportunities that can guide your decisions.

6. Mutual Benefit: Consider how being a secret board member would benefit the individual. What could they gain from this relationship? Mutual benefit can make them more likely to accept the role and make it more fruitful on both ends.

7. Availability: Ensure that potential secret board members have the time and willingness to engage in this capacity. Some board members may require weekly meetings while others may only need to check in annually. In any case, ensure that

they have the availability from the get-go to maximize the effectiveness of your board in the long run.

8. Compatibility: Assess whether potential secret board members' values, ethics, and approaches align with your own. Compatibility will foster effective communication and understanding. However, be sure to maintain a balance between compatibility and leaving your comfort zone! It's always a good idea to align with your board members on core values and how they operate, but it's also crucial to pick board members who you feel can stretch your skill set and potentially challenge you.

9. Openness to Feedback: Look for individuals who are open to giving and receiving feedback. A willingness to engage in candid discussions is crucial for the success of this arrangement.

10. Evaluation Period: Consider starting with a trial period to assess the compatibility and effectiveness of a board member. This gives both parties the chance to determine if the arrangement is beneficial.

11. Legal and Ethical Considerations: Depending on the nature of your relationship and the information shared, consult legal and ethical guidelines to ensure that the arrangement respects confidentiality and privacy rules. Sometimes, a standard NDA and contract is the best way to go!

12. Balanced Perspectives: Strive to create a board with a balance of skills, experiences, and viewpoints to ensure well-rounded advice and insights.

As you brainstorm the best way to build your board, dive deeper into the following questions:

- What do I already have in my life?
- What do I need more of in my life?

- What do I need less of in my life?
- Why do I want this?
- Who else will this affect? How?
- What will I do about it?
- What resources do I need? Who can help me?
- When will I do it?
- When will I know I'm there? What concrete evidence will I experience?
- How will I keep myself accountable and motivated?

The Wheel in Motion

Shelley Poovey, a Reiki Master and energy healer with over a decade of experience, integrates subtle energy work with peak performance coaching, empowering clients to overcome obstacles with greater ease. Passionate about teaching others to harness the power of subtle energy, she helps people tap into their inner potential, transforming challenges into opportunities for growth and success. Learn more at www.bodyatune.com.

After looking at the roles and responsibilities of a personal board member …

1. *In what way did the results of the Wheel of Life change how you think about seeking support?*

   The wheel of life (WOL) serves as a mind map, a schematic vision board. I tend to be someone who focuses on spirituality, and the WOL made me think about my satisfaction in other areas.

   The WOL supports spiritual practice, sacred geometry, and archetypal representation, eg: in relationships of distancing or developing.

The WOL enables attraction of the vision in that area to become stronger in my life.

2. *What category of the Wheel has a board member played a role with and can you provide specifics?*

   My secret board member is Shahida Arabi, author of **The Highly Sensitive Person's Guide to Dealing with Toxic People.** *This helps me focus on the relationships part of my wheel and address people-pleasing behavior. It helped me identify toxic behaviors, and I could measure the change of satisfaction through the wheel of life.*

3. *Can you share how strategically thinking about roles and responsibilities has influenced your relationship with your board members?*

   The WOL helped illuminate relationships. I've become more strategic in the relationships area with my inner circle and outer circle and add outcomes—relationship, marriage etc.

Your Next Steps

Identify your board members for each area of your *Wheel of Life.*

1. What role will each of them play?
2. What change might you want after working with this board member?
3. Can you state what you bring to the table in the relationship?
4. You may have rated yourself a 10 in a category, and who could you add to broaden your perspective?

Fill out the names of possible board members for each category:

1. Fun
2. Finance
3. Friends and Family
4. Growth Mindset
5. Personal and Professional Growth
6. Relationships
7. Spirituality
8. Wellbeing

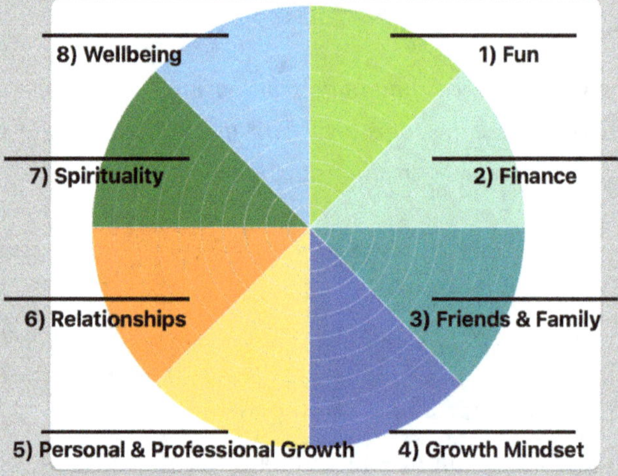

Figure 4.1 Wheel of Life Board Members

Chapter 5

GROWTH MINDSET

> *"Many times, we need to make friends with growth-minded people,*
> *including an accountability partner, an organized peer, and*
> *a mentor. These 'partners in progress' will help you achieve*
> *success by discussing and taking action towards your goals*
> *while holding each other accountable."*
>
> —Asuni LadyZeal

So far, we've explored people you look up to in Chapter 1, possible secret board members in Chapter 2, completed the *Wheel of Life* in Chapter 3, and identified areas of the *Wheel* you might want to work on in Chapter 4. You may already have possible board members for each category of your *Wheel of Life*. In any case, before approaching a prospective board member, let's explore a growth mindset.

If you've made it this far just by choosing to read this book, you likely already have a growth mindset. Most importantly, you're brainstorming how to put together the perfect personal board of directors! The two go hand in hand—by building the ideal board for you, you'll have the people you need by your side to nurture your growth mindset. But what *is* a growth mindset and why does it matter for us?

In chapter 1, (Stacy) wrote about my early introduction to the Silva Method at age sixteen. The practice made such a memorable impact on my view of mental training that when I experience a challenging time or situation, I remind myself that I have this tool to use. The Silva Method is a self-improvement method developed by mind scientist Jose Silva after years of research in the 1960s.

This technique empowers you to achieve your goals, enhance your wellbeing, and unlock the secrets of your consciousness. Various studies, research projects, and practical applications have demonstrated its efficacy in improving mental, emotional, and physical wellbeing. This has since led to other techniques such as a positive mindset and a growth mindset.

The term growth mindset was coined by American psychologist Professor Carol Dweck in her 2006 book *Mindset: The New Psychology of Success*. She describes two main ways people think about intelligence or ability. They have either a fixed mindset or a growth mindset.

- In a **fixed mindset**, people believe that their intelligence is fixed and static. In other words, you're born with it.

- In a **growth mindset**, people believe that their intelligence and talents can be improved through effort and learning.

We should also distinguish the difference between a positive mindset and a growth mindset. They are related but distinct concepts. A positive mindset focuses on reframing a challenging situation and looking for ways to see a situation through a "glass half full approach," while a growth mindset emphasizes fully understanding the situation, identifying the actual problem, and seeking opportunities for learning and development in the journey towards identifying solutions.

What Is a Growth Mindset?

"This growth mindset is based on the belief that your basic qualities are things you can cultivate through your efforts. Although people may differ in every which way—in their initial talents and aptitudes, interests, or temperaments—everyone can change and grow through application and experience."

—Carol Dweck

Instead of repeating fixed thoughts, try affirming your goal with a growth statement. The following table shows some frequent self-talk statements that are self-limiting and offer a reframing of the goal as a growth statement.

Wheel of Life Areas	Fixed Mindset Statements *"Instead of"*	Growth Mindset Statements *"Try thinking"*	Growth Mindset Statements with Rewards *"Add your Reward for achieving your goal"*
Fun	I'm just too tired	I chose one fun activity a week	I choose one fun activity a week and I enjoy laughter
Finance	I don't know how to manage money well	I seek out financial strategies	I learn about financial management strategies, create a plan, and I feel in control
Friends and Family	No one is interested in my opinion	I learn new ways to communicate	I learn new ways to communicate, and I foster closer bonds with friends/family

Growth Mindset	I don't like change	I am open to growth mindset activities	I focus on growth mindset activities, and I feel empowered
Personal & Professional growth	I just can't do this technology project	I am open to embracing technology	I focus on learning new technologies, and I feel accomplished
Relationships	I have a hard time connecting with others	I use active listening to deepen my relationships	I use active listening to deepen my relationships, and I feel more connected to others
Spirituality	I give up	I have faith and trust	I have faith and trust in my spiritual practice, and I feel at peace
Wellbeing	I have too many health problems	I am healthier	I practice self-care daily, and I feel healthier

Table 5.1 Sample Fixed and Growth Mindset Statements & Rewards

Ten Ways to Develop a Growth Mindset

According to Dr. Dweck's research, no one has an entirely fixed or an entirely growth mindset; most are somewhere in the middle. However, we can continually build and nurture our growth mindset. Let's look into ten ways to develop a growth mindset. As you read these tips, keep in mind the ones that resonate with you as they may become some of your main goals while building your board.

1. Identify your own mindset.

By considering how you currently approach challenges, either at work or in education, you can determine your current mindset. For example, you can ask yourself whether you would say things to yourself like, *I'm a natural people person* or *I've learned to work well with people*? Or would you say, *They are a natural leader,* or *They worked their way up to the leadership role?*

2. Look at your own improvements.

Think about something you're better at now than you were in the past. What did you previously find difficult? Why does it feel easier now? And how did you achieve such a change? If you build the right board, satisfying growth like this can start to become your new normal.

3. Review the success of others.

Try to think about something that you've seen someone else do against the odds. Think about how they achieved their success and what this says about their ability to develop their capabilities. Of course, once again, if you have the right people on your board, reviewing *and* getting inspired by their successes can become routine for you and help you in your own goals!

4. Seek feedback.

Whether you've been successful in a project or not, seeking feedback is a good way to develop a growth mindset. Others may give you insight into where you've developed or what needs improvement. In turn, this can help you to set goals for improvement.

5. Harness the power of "yet."

The concept of "yet" is one that Dr. Dweck spoke about during a TEDx talk. Essentially, this part of a fixed mindset is about realizing that there will be skills or subjects that you're not good at yet. However, with work and perseverance, you can improve in these areas. This is what building a board is all about—oftentimes, leveraging expertise. This brings us to our next point …

6. Learn something new.

Try a completely new activity and challenge yourself to learn something that you're not already good at. You could start with learning a new language, picking up an instrument, or understanding the basics of economics.

7. Make mistakes.

You're not going to get everything right the first time trying. Allow yourself to make errors and then learn from those missteps. Rather than thinking that mistakes equal ineptitude, think of them as part of the learning process. The more you learn, the more chances you'll have to make mistakes, but you'll also optimize your chances of success.

8. Be kind to yourself.

Rather than scolding yourself for your errors, try and identify how you'd treat someone else in your situation. If someone were to fail at a task you know inside out, would you tell them they're useless or encourage them to learn?

9. Look at examples.

If you're striving to develop a growth mindset, it can help to look at those who already embody one. Whether they're examples from experts such as Dr. Dweck or through looking at people you already know, there are opportunities to learn from others. Examine what they do and how they approach challenges and think about how you can apply similar tactics.

10. Set realistic goals.

As we've explored already, there are many determinants of success. Personality, intelligence, circumstance, and other factors can all contribute. However, by setting clear goals that provide a motivating challenge, you can work towards success.

Strategies for Nurturing Growth Mindset

Our students and colleagues have shared some strategies to develop a growth mindset from their learnings:

- Take ownership of your attitude
- Develop a personal mission
- Clarify your vision and values
- Cultivate a sense of purpose
- View challenges as opportunities
- Try different learning methods
- Recognize steps for improvement
- Learn from others
- Celebrate the journey
- Replace failure with persistence
- Reinforce growth with others
- Use positive powerful action words

Why Does Mindset Matter?

In 1988, Dr. Dweck first presented a research-based model to show the impact of mindset. She showed how a person's mindset sets the stage for either performance goals or learning goals. A person with a performance goal might be worried about looking smart all the time and avoid challenging work. On the other hand, a person with a learning goal will pursue interesting and challenging tasks to learn more.

In subsequent studies, Dr. Dweck found that people's theories about their own intelligence had a significant impact on their motivation, effort, and approach to challenges. Those who believe their abilities are malleable are more likely to embrace challenges and persist despite failure.

How Do You Find a Growth-Mindset Board Member?

People with a growth mindset genuinely want to expand their knowledge and are open to opportunities. Potential board members with a growth mindset are devoted to seeking opportunities and will help you to go and grow further. In fact, individuals with a growth mindset:

- Seek to continuously evaluate and improve their work and personal life.

- Are typically high achievers, tend to innovate, and may take calculated risks.

- Take classes and pursue outside education to enhance their skills.

- Cultivate and maintain their personal relationships and work to better themselves outside of their professional life.

Stacy's Journey to Add the Right Board Member with a Growth Mindset

When I thought about my category of the *Wheel of Life* most in need of a board member, I was digging deep for secret board members, friends, and family for financial wellness. I was coming up a bit short but knew I wanted someone with a growth mindset. I found Dow Jane and started taking online classes with their financial coaches.

I really forced myself to visualize my optimal ending point for financial wellness and started with a vision board of what that looks like. Remember: It's all about setting specific goals and then using your board to reverse-engineer the way to get there.

Figure 5.1 Stacy's Pinterest Board for Finance Category

I was determined to live in a growth mindset and learn what I could to gather momentum and accountability. In the first week with Dow Jane, one of my assignments was to create a positive mindset about money by looking at neutral and positive words and creating positive money mantras like these:

- I can learn what I don't know when it comes to my finances.

- I can build wealth through small decisions and actions that I make each day.

- I am living debt-free in retirement.

This is where my friend and co-author comes in. Dr. Leena is a role model for a positive mindset and as one of my personal board members, she is well-positioned to set me up for success.

So, I made a plan to take a potential board member to lunch. My friend is a financial planner. I wanted to share what my plan was and hopefully get validation that I was on the right track, and it started with a growth mindset. I already wanted to improve my personal life. I was also taking classes to enhance my knowledge and skills. Turns out, that is exactly what I was looking for. Someone who was also growing each day and not someone who was just an expert in their field.

Leena's Journey to Add the Right Board Member with a Growth Mindset

As we write this chapter, I've exceeded my five-year prognosis, following an aggressive adenocarcinoma in 2019. (I consider myself a cancer thriver, not a survivor) Although I'm known for a positive mindset, this example shows how my chosen board member reinforced my growth mindset through self-care.

My self-care/health board member came into my life over a decade ago and is co-author Dr. Stacy Gomes. Stacy has such a natural way of checking in and offering support. To give you some background, whenever we meet, she not only asks me how self-care is going, but when she hears I'm taking action to achieve my goal, she has a silent yet palpable energy of support and motivation.

She keeps focused on maintaining a growth mindset without even realizing it, just by asking about my vision and goals and celebrates even the smallest of steps. She will never know how keeping me on track for five years after my diagnosis (and more) in mind and body has literally supported my now thriving state of being. I feel blessed to have her on my personal board of directors.

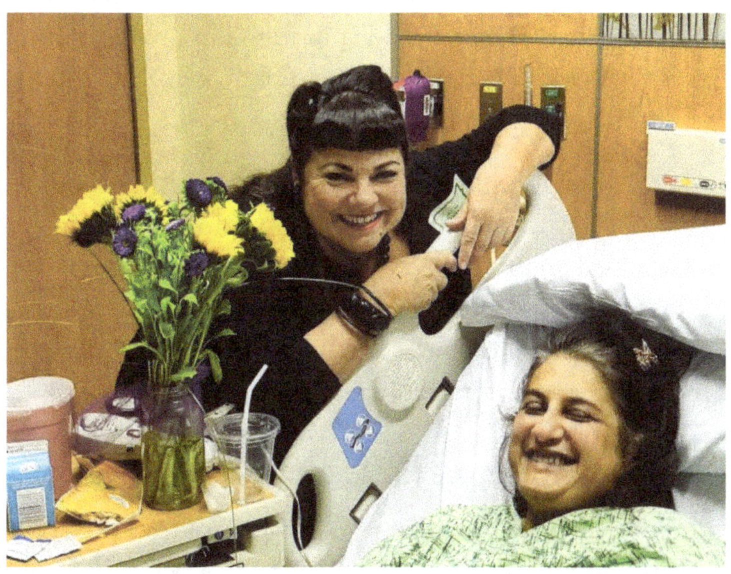

The Growth-Mindset Seat on Your Board of Directors

Let's start with the growth-mindset attributes of your board members.

As you can likely tell by our stories, a growth mindset doesn't mean ignoring or denying the existence of problems or negative emotions. Instead, it's about working to find solutions and growth opportunities. This is where your growth-mindset board member can be worth their weight in gold.

Cultivating a growth mindset is a development goal that can lead to increased wellbeing and improved life satisfaction. It's a mindset that can be developed and nurtured through your growth-mindset board members as well as embracing positive self-talk, recognizing when those pesky negative thoughts come in, and adopting positive affirmations to achieve your dream goals!

Ten Steps to Positive Growth Statements

Creating positive growth statements with rewards can be a powerful tool to affirm a more positive outlook and drive desired life changes. Our mind is influenced by repetition, emotional resonance, and belief. Research indicates that the repetition of positive statements helps form new neural pathways in the brain. Some experts claim that it takes 10,000 repetitions to form a new neural pathway—essentially, a new belief or thought pattern. This process, known as neuroplasticity, allows for changes in thoughts and behaviors over time, which is what growth mindset is all about!

Here's a step-by-step guide on how to create positive growth statements with rewards that support growth mindset:

1. **Identify Your Goal(s):** Begin by clarifying your goal areas from your *Wheel of Life*. Whether it's self-confidence, health, relationships, abundance, or success, you need to know what

you want to achieve with your growth statement(s). Consider making a vision board like I did with my financial goals (Stacy) to identify your particular objectives.

2. **Frame Your Statement Positively**: Phrase your statement in a positive and in the _present tense_. Avoid those more fixed words like "don't," "can't," or "won't." Instead, focus on what you want not what you want to avoid or fear. For example, say, "I am confident and capable" instead of "I am afraid."

3. **Be Specific:** Make your statements specific to your goals. This helps your mind understand exactly what you're working toward. For instance, "I make healthy food choices to nourish my body" is more specific than "I am healthy."

4. **Use Emotion and Visualization:** Engage your emotions by including feelings and visualization. Describe how you will feel when you achieve your goals. This connects the statement with your emotions, making it more powerful.

   For example, "I feel joy and fulfillment and I achieve my dreams." You may see yourself as a superhero with a cape and powerful tools, or in armor plating with bullets and negativity simply rebounding off your suit.

5. **Keep it Concise:** Keep your statements short and concise. This makes them easy to remember, repeat, and or visualize throughout the day. If you can repeat your statements without needing to read them from a notepad, then your growth statements are resonating well as a part of you.

6. **Make Your Statements Personal:** Use "I" statements, this helps you connect with them on a deeper level.

   For instance, say "I attract positive abundance" instead of "You attract positive abundance."

You can also make them more personal by phrasing them in the way that you typically speak! Sometimes, the most impactful affirmations are the ones that have you feeling like you're telling the good news to a friend.

7. **Ensure you have a reward**: The reward needs to be well-balanced and proportional to the goal. Think of the goal on one side of a scale and the reward on another. A small goal with a large reward creates imbalance, and a large goal with only a small reward may reduce self-motivation to reach the reward.

   "I attract positive abundance, and I feel successful."

8. **Repeat Regularly:** Repeat and visualize your statements daily to accept and internalize them. Consistency is key. If it doesn't feel right, modify your goal or reward language until the statement truly reflects and resonates with you.

9. **Use Tools:** You can enhance the effectiveness of your positive growth statements by writing them down, pasting them as a note on the bathroom mirror and repeat while brushing your teeth, or by the bedside, creating vision boards, recording your growth statements, listening to them while you are relaxed or meditating and visualizing yourself having achieved your goal and seeing the outcome of your reward.

10. **Believe in Your Statement:** To engage your mind fully, you must believe in the statement you're repeating. If you have doubts, work on addressing and changing your attitude towards the goal area. (If it's what you really want for yourself, then address any attitudinal barriers first). Be patient and persistent, it takes time to nurture a growth-mindset attitude.

Continuing to Build Your Growth Mindset

Review and Adjust: Periodically review your statements and adjust them as your goals evolve. Sometimes growth statements may work for you and last over decades. For example, "I have mind-body-spirit balance, and I feel at peace." Other times, it may serve you for the short term until achieved, such as, "I embrace learning new technologies and am more confident in my work."

Monitor Your Thoughts: Pay attention to your thoughts throughout the day. If you catch yourself thinking in a fixed, negative, or self-sabotaging way, replace those thoughts with your growth statement and a reward for getting there.

Remember that creating positive growth statements is a personal process. Create them to your specific needs, goals, and or areas of your *Wheel of Life*. Over time, you'll start to see changes in your thoughts and attitudes.

Cultivating a growth mindset is an ongoing process. It's about developing a habit of thinking in a more positive and constructive way. Be consistent in your efforts, and over time, you can train your mind to default to a more positive outlook. Finding the right board member with a growth mindset can be much easier once you complete your own Growth Mindset Assessment at the end of this chapter!

Strengthen Board Bonds by Completing the "Feedback" Loop

When sharing with Stacy how she played a key role in my self-care and cancer recovery, her first comment was, "Oh, I didn't know I played that role." Though your secret board members may never truly know how they serve you, that can be the case for your chosen board members, too. By sharing with them the impact they've had on you, you can deepen your relationship with a board member and how valuable they truly are—whether physically close or at a distance.

Wheel in Motion

Dr. Greg Lane, DACM, LAc, is a Doctor of Acupuncture and Chinese Medicine, program director for Integral Health at the California Institute of Human Science and Longevity, and Clinical Director at Lumati. He integrates traditional Chinese medical wisdom with cutting-edge technology with health care coaching using the Wheel of Life. His professional experience spans over 31 years of direct patient care and higher education.

Life can be overwhelming. Sometimes it can feel like a cascading waterfall of insurmountable obstacles where nothing goes one's way. I have a patient, let's call her Jane, who is a fifty-five-year-old woman working in nursing. Specifically, she's an RN who works in hospice care, one of the most challenging segments of the healthcare system.

I've been seeing Jane for over a year now, and every session we work together, she's extremely stressed-out, angry, and resentful due to the nature of her work. She describes the families that she works with as nasty and vindictive, often placing blame and unrealistic expectations on her for the death and dying process of their loved ones.

This deep dissatisfaction in her work environment and relations have caused such a significant negative impact on her, that the only way to help her out of the avalanche of persistent negative thoughts and emotions was to "chunk" her life into separate buckets so that it is more manageable. The only way to eat an elephant is one bite at a time, right? We used The Wheel of Life to chunk down bite-sized portions into relationships, spirituality, finances, work, fun, and health to assist her in making some real changes and breaking her cycle of despair.

What she came up with was a plan to actively seek new employment and pursue new training so that she could be hirable in utilization management, which would provide her the same level of income and more peace in her working environment. She has not yet transitioned, but at least she sees a way out of her predicament. The Wheel of Life was very helpful for her to not be oppressed by the entirety of her life, and to take control of her own destiny.

Homework Step 5: Create a growth mindset to attract the right board members.

Complete the Carol Dweck's Growth vs. Fixed Mindset Assessment:

bit.ly/3Ks9kwE

To what actions are you willing to commit to support your growth mindset?

Chapter 6

APPLYING THE WHEEL OF LIFE TO CURATING YOUR BOARD

"The journey of a thousand miles begins with one step."

—Lao Tzu

Keep the End in Mind

Let's go back to Covey's second habit of *7 Habits of Highly Effective People* … "Keep The End in Mind." Why do we want a personal board of directors? Who do you lean on in areas that you want to improve? Do you have a system, process, or plan to "sharpen your saw?" Don't forget, if YOU haven't chosen your board, your board will choose you!

Board members that you didn't consciously pick & choose can strongly influence and sidetrack you! On the other hand, if you use this approach to select your own board members and place them into relevant *Wheel of Life* categories, you can delegate priorities effectively. For instance, if a well-intentioned board member does sidetrack you, you can say, "Thanks so much for your suggestions. I've been working with one of my board members who has strongly encouraged me to do XYZ based on their many years of experience in this area."

A New Way of Viewing Your Personal Board of Directors

Now that you understand the difference between a traditional board of directors and a personal board of directors, let's review some new thinking on how your board members can help you. They can:

- Help you gain clarity on your next best steps in life.
- Take you to another level of understanding in a topic/area you are focused on becoming an expert in.
- Help you recognize and eliminate old, self-sabotaging habits.
- Break down daunting goals into realistic and manageable steps.
- Ensure long-term goals remain in sight as your focus expands.
- Help you prepare for what's ahead.
- Support and motivate you.
- Ask you the questions that you don't ask (or avoid asking) yourself.
- Challenge you to new ways of thinking.
- Support your ongoing progress.
- Be a sounding board for new ideas.
- Support you to overcome obstacles.
- Keep you accountable and committed to your goals.
- Help you maintain a growth mindset.
- Celebrate your successes!

Secret Board Members

Start with your secret board members. Go back and look at your list. Why did you pick them? Let's review how they can help:

- They provide valuable knowledge/experience/content you need.
- They stay up on current thinking in their field.
- They do homework for you. (They've been there.)

- They don't judge you because they don't know you.
- They provide inspiration.
- They can motivate you to try something new with no pressure.
- You won't feel obligated to report to them.
- You can follow them without them knowing.

Curate Your Board Using the *Wheel of Life*

You've completed the *Wheel of Life,* and you see the areas that you may want to work on. What's your next step? Your next step is "getting the right people on your bus." So how do you find them? Who are they? What are they doing for you? Hopefully, you've already started making a list and connecting them to your *Wheel of Life* categories.

Align Your Board Members' Roles with Your Goals/Categories

Remember, your personal board of directors can work for you in a variety of ways, depending on your goal(s) and need(s). The entire purpose of curating your board is to ensure you have a *personalized* system set in place to help you reach your goals. Make sure you are clear on what you are seeking to change with their support. Here are ways board members can support your *Wheel of Life*:

1. Mentorship: A board member with more experience and wisdom in your field can provide guidance and advice on how to navigate your career or personal development.

2. Networking: A board member with a large network of contacts can help you make valuable connections and open doors for you.

3. Accountability: Board members can help keep you accountable to your goals and provide motivation and support along the way.

4. Financial Guidance: A board member with expertise in finance can help you with budgeting, investment, or financial planning.

5. Emotional Support: Board members can be a source of emotional support and encouragement during challenging times.

6. Skill Development: Board members can provide opportunities for you to develop new skills or gain new experiences that will help you achieve your goals.

Nurturing Growth Mindset to Balance Your Wheel

People with a growth mindset genuinely want to expand their knowledge and are open to opportunities. Potential board members with a growth mindset are devoted to seeking opportunities and will help you to go and grow further. In fact, individuals with a growth mindset:

- Seek to continuously evaluate and improve their work and personal life.
- Are typically high achievers, tend to innovate, and may take calculated risks.
- Take trainings/workshops or courses, pursuing outside education to enhance their skills.
- Cultivate and maintain their personal relationships and work to better themselves outside of their professional lives (keeping their wheel in motion).

Let's look at strategies for nurturing a growth mindset based on our work with students and colleagues:

- Take ownership of your attitude
- Develop and live your personal mission
- Clarify your vision and core values
- Cultivate a sense of purpose
- View challenges as opportunities
- Embrace different learning methods
- Recognize and celebrate steps of improvement

- Act as a lifelong learner by learning from others
- Replace failure with persistence
- Celebrate the journey with all its ups and downs
- Reinforce growth with others
- Use positive, powerful action words

Cultivating a growth mindset is an ongoing process. Don't get discouraged. It has been reported in 2005, that the National Science Foundation published an article summarizing research on human thoughts per day, and found that the average person has about 12,000 to 60,000 thoughts per day. Of those thousands of thoughts, 80% were negative, and 95% were exactly the same repetitive thoughts as the day before. You can write your positive statements on your phone, and put them by your bedside, in the bathroom, or on the refrigerator. Put them in any place where you can see them and repeat them several times a day. What actions were you willing to commit to in support of your growth mindset?

Step 6: Make contact with potential board members and describe what area they might help with.

How Could You Ask Someone to Be on Your Board?

Start with your existing network (1st-degree connections), asking for a warm intro (2nd-degree connections), sending a personalized cold email (3rd+-degree connections), or offering to help the other person.

Send them a text or email and describe your desire to create a personal board of directors. If they respond favorably, ask to schedule a phone call or coffee chat to catch up and share what's on your mind.

How Often Do You Need to Connect?

If you don't run into any of your members on a day-to-day basis, aim to touch base semi-annually or annually, more often if your situation dictates. When in doubt, *ask* them if they have a preferred method of staying in contact, e.g. text, email, social media, private chat, zoom, in-person, etc.

In your update, share your progress since you last connected, referencing specific ways you incorporated their feedback and what the results were. This will help them see that their time was well-spent and led to measurable impact. And of course, always express gratitude.

Your Life Is Evolving. Should Your Board Evolve, Too?

Yes! As your life evolves, so too will your board. Since your personal board of directors is not a formal entity, there is no need to "hire" or "fire" anyone (in fact, we don't recommend this!) However, it may be that some members stick around for the long haul, while others' expertise or career advice is no longer relevant to your new goals/categories. The important thing is that you have a list of trusted advisors that you can count on at any point in your life, even if your board itself changes.

Six Final Steps to Build Your Dream Support Team

All you need to curate your personal board of directors are these six steps:

- ***Step 1:*** *Make a list of people you look up to who have succeeded in something that impresses you.*
- ***Step 2:*** *Identify "secret" board members, people you know or follow that will help you improve.*
- ***Step 3:*** *Complete the Wheel of Life, and identify three categories you want to focus on.*
- ***Step 4:*** *Identify your board members for each area of your Wheel of Life.*
- ***Step 5:*** *Create a growth mindset to attract the right board members.*

- ***Step 6:*** *Make contact with your potential board members, and describe what area they might help with.*

If you've been seeking to bring more purpose and balance into your life, this book is your all-in-one guide. We invite you to keep it by your side! These six steps offer a clear path to achieving harmony across all areas of your life without sacrificing one for another. By taking small, consistent actions each day, you can build a powerful network of support through your personal board of directors.

People are naturally inclined to invest in those with a positive and promising outlook. By being intentional and thoughtful in nurturing these relationships, you'll create a lasting and supportive network that will propel you toward sustained success and fulfillment for years to come.

How to Get More Help

Who's on Your Board guides you in developing and tracking progress on your desired life goals (using the *Wheel of Life*) and creating a team of personal board members. Learn how to bring your dreams to reality through this quick, easy, simple process of powering up to live your best life.

Gain insight from the authors through a free training. Learn how the creation of positive affirmations can amplify your growth mindset in a free download. Understand the role of the growth mindset in creating your personal Board of Directors. Growth mindset can create a winning combination for you to maximize your *Wheel in Motion*, achieve your goals, and craft the life you've always envisioned and deserve.

www.WhosOnYourBoard.com/bookdownload

ACKNOWLEDGMENTS

This book would not be possible without the boards that we have been on (ACCAHC, ACIH, AIHM, CCAOM, UCSD CIM, AMTA, NCBTMB) and guidance from our own personal board members. To our friends (in no particular order) who have read drafts, provided valuable feedback, and pushed us to keep writing on this journey. To our editor, Alicia Wilcox, whose vibrant, youthful feedback was a needed filter for our stiff, older style of writing, and our Software Engineer, Miles Exner, who patiently designed our *Wheel of Life* and QR code.

Marilyn Allen

Beau Anderson

Leon Chaitow (RIP)

Susana Clark

Ian Drysdale

Liza Goldblatt

Mykel Golden

Delanie Gomes

Ben Greenfield

Louise Hay

Julie Hunt

Kellie Knight

Greg Lane

Eunice & Roy Low

Rita Mitra (RIP)

Clarissa Patterson

Joe Tafur

Solange Vandenburg

Dale & Ted Wallace

Jeffrey Zlotnik

ABOUT THE AUTHORS

Stacy L. Gomes, EdD, MEd

Her life-long attention on self-care quickly gained momentum and structure in 2007. What started out as a binder of categories for new year's resolutions with her good friend and board member Marilyn Allen grew into organized and ongoing self-improvement with the *Wheel of Life*. The enhanced benefit of adding board members to each area allowed intentional conversations about ways to improve. As a result, she was inspired to teach her doctoral students to build their own personal board of directors to help them with their self-care and to stay balanced while building a career.

Dr. Gomes is currently Provost at California Institute of Human Science and spent twenty-eight years as Vice President of Academic Affairs at Pacific College of Health and Science. She is a professional educator that has coached and mentored thousands of clinicians in integrative whole-health care. She prioritizes self-care and self-improvement for herself and others and has used versions of the *Wheel of Life* to create balance in her own life and gather her own board members to guide her on this path. She believes and teaches her students that we are better aligned to serve others when our own life is in balance. As a member of several different boards, she understands the focus on financial stability and growth and brings this unique perspective to our personal lives using the *Wheel of Life*.

Leena S. Guptha, DO, MBA, PhD

Leena Susan Guptha is a clinician, educator, professional certified coach (PCC) and lifelong learner whose journey embodies the very principles she teaches—balance, maximizing human potential, and living a purposeful life with joy and happiness. Drawing from her diverse background in osteopathic and naturopathic medicine, acupuncture, business, coaching, health and human performance, and education, Dr. Guptha has dedicated her life to helping others discover and utilize their highest potential.

Her work is deeply informed by the *Wheel of Life*, a tool she has used personally and professionally to guide goal setting, foster resilience, and promote health and wellbeing, which has all been possible through the support of her personal board members. From clinical practice to international stages in Sri Lanka, Great Britain, Italy, and the United States, Dr. Guptha empowers individuals to set meaningful goals across every domain of life—for health, career, relationships, and spiritual awareness—cultivating balance and transformation along the way.

This book is a reflection of her journey—multidimensional, intentional, and grounded in the belief that with board of directors everyone can create a life of fulfillment.

REFERENCES

Bonporte, J. *The Secret to Making Board Meetings Suck Less*. 2015.

Carnegie, Dale. *How to Win Friends and Influence People*. New York: Simon & Schuster, 1936.

Coelho, Paulo. *Manual of the Warrior of Light*. New York: HarperCollins, 2003.

Coelho, Paulo. *The Alchemist*. San Francisco: HarperOne, 1988.

Collins, Jim. *Good to Great: Why Some Companies Make the Leap … and Others Don't*. New York: HarperBusiness, 2001.

Connell, Emily Davis. *How to Recruit, Engage, and Retain Millennial Board Members*. New York: Candid, 2018.

Covey, Stephen R. *The 7 Habits of Highly Effective People: Powerful Lessons in Personal Change*. New York: Free Press, 1989.

Dweck, Carol S. *Mindset: The New Psychology of Success*. New York: Random House, 2006.

George, Bill. *True North: Discover Your Authentic Leadership*. San Francisco: Jossey-Bass, 2007.

Govenda. "Millennials in the Boardroom." Blog post, 2018. https://www.govenda.com/blog/millennials-in-the-boardroom

Hill, Napoleon. *Think and Grow Rich*. New York: The Ralston Society, 1937.

Perlman, A., B. Horrigan, E. Goldblatt, V. Maizes, and B. Kligler. *Pebble in the Pond: How Integrative Leadership Can Bring About Transformational Change*. Durham, NC: Duke Integrative Medicine, 2014.

Silva Method. "Home Page." Accessed August 26, 2025. https://silva-method.com